Harriet Lane

America's First Lady

Milton Stern

Milton Stern
miltonstern@harrietlane.net
www.harrietlane.net

Cover Design: Abdulzatar Kuku (kuku@mrkuku.com)
Interior Book Design: Milton Stern (miltonstern@harrietlane.net)

Front Cover Photograph: Harriet Lane in Her Inaugural Gown,
March 4, 1857, courtesy of the Wadner-Spahr Library, Dickinson
College, Carlisle, Pennsylvania. Background Portrait: James
Buchanan's Wheatland by Milton Stern, October 2003.

Photo Credits: Every effort has been made to identify copyright
holders, and necessary permission and reprint agreements have
been obtained for all photographes included in this publication
with the exception of those from the author's personal collection.
In the event of an oversight, corrections will be made in the next
edition.

Other Titles by Milton Stern

On Tuesday, They Play Mah Jongg
(1985)
America's Bachelor President and the First Lady (2004)

Dedication

To the memory of Harriet Lane Johnston (May 9, 1830 – July 3, 1903), "The Lady of the White House, and by courtesy, the First Lady of the Land," whose optimism and zest for life is an inspiration to everyone.

To Serena Rose Elizabeth Montgomery, my toy parti-poodle, for her patience as I sat in front of the computer writing my second book.

To Sharon Gillespie, my editor, whose books I wish to edit some day soon.

Acknowledgements

Thank you to Katie Cassarly and the James Buchanan Foundation for the Preservation of Wheatland for their support for both my books and their assistance in locating photographs of Harriet Lane and James Buchanan.

Thank you to Jim Gerencser, Archivist of the Wadner-Spahr Library, Dickinson College, Carlisle, Pennsylvania, for his assistance in locating the recently discovered photograph of Harriet Lane in her inaugural gown (front cover), along with the Lily Macalester letters.

Thank you to Richard Sorenson of the Smithsonian American Art Museum for his assistance in locating photographs from the Harriet Lane Johnston Collection.

Thank you to Dawn Bonner of the Mount Vernon Ladies' Association for her assistance in locating photographs of Lily Macalester.

Thank you to David Baker of St. Albans School for his assistance in locating the photograph of Harriet Lane Johnston taken in 1898.

Thank you to the staff of the Kiplinger Library of the City Museum, Washington, D.C.

Thank you to the Library of Congress staff.

Harriet Lane
America's First Lady

Milton Stern

Contents

A note about the transcripts of original correspondence, speeches, and other personal notes: When including the text of any official or personal written correspondence, the author retained the original spelling, capitalization, grammar and punctuation throughout this book. Necessary corrections are indicated by open and close brackets.

Preface

In October 2003, I visited Wheatland, the Lancaster, Pennsylvania, estate of James Buchanan, fifteenth President of the United States. As I completed research there on my first historical biography, based on the life of Buchanan, one of the staff suggested I write a separate book about Harriet Lane, Buchanan's niece who played such a key role in his life during his presidency and beyond. Though I dedicated one third of *America's Bachelor President and the First Lady* to the story of the first woman to be referred to as First Lady, I really had no intention of writing another book about Buchanan and Lane, as I was already in the middle of researching another nineteenth century president; but I could not get Harriet Lane's story out of my mind. Every time I found material on my intended subject, I would somehow come across another interesting piece on Lane.

So I wondered: "Had I done her justice in the first book?" "Did I include all there was about her story?" "Would people really get to know the most admired woman of her time?" I pulled out the materials I had gathered while researching Buchanan's life and started reading through those items I had not included. That was when I realized there was so much more to the story of Harriet Lane.

I revisited the sources of my initial research: The Library of Congress, James Buchanan's Wheatland, The Wadner-Spahr Library at Dickinson College, The Pennsylvania Historical Society, Johns Hopkins University, and the archives of *The New York Times*. Then, I researched the archives of *The Washington Post* and discovered an entire part of Harriet Lane that had not been explored — the last two decades of her life. Hardly a week went by during the Washington social seasons between 1886 and 1902 when Harriet Lane Johnston was not mentioned in the society pages.

However, it was her Last Will and Testament that fascinated me more than anything. By the second page, I realized what an historical document I was reading. Her generosity sustained a pediatric hospital and a national gallery, and established a school, along with many other significant bequests. Of course, there was the entire section dedicated to the

James Buchanan Monument, of which the details alone were fascinating. While looking for news about the monument, I stumbled over a series of articles about the controversy surrounding the bequest and the nasty comments made about President James Buchanan on the floors of both houses of Congress, by lawmakers who were born after his term as president ended. I had always assumed that she left the $100,000 for the monument and Congress accepted it without question. I never realized how close it came to never being built. More importantly, what was revealed was that although her uncle was a polarizing figure, her character and grace, even beyond death, was what saved the project.

Writing this book has been quite moving at times. After researching someone's life so thoroughly, reading her letters, other correspondence, the obituaries and articles, and then seeing her misspelled name in the City Directory of Washington, D.C., it is difficult not to get emotionally involved.

Finally, I appreciated the feedback from readers of my previous book on Buchanan and Lane, and I have incorporated some of their suggestions into the format of this book.

For one, readers will notice that I have included pertinent excerpts of correspondence in the chapters. For those wishing to read the entire text, I have included complete letters in Annex D. Other readers have asked me to include photos. I have included in this book photos that I originally submitted for the first, but were not included. Also, through the generosity of the James Buchanan Foundation for the Preservation of Wheatland, I have included additional pictures of Harriet Lane and James Buchanan. In addition, the Wadner-Spahr Library at Dickinson College has generously given me permission to use a recently discovered photograph of Harriet Lane in her famous inaugural gown.

I truly hope I have done justice to the memory of Harriet Lane, who deserves a place among the most important women in American history.

There is an interviewer on television, who always asks, "If you could throw a dinner party with anyone dead or alive, whom would you invite?" My answer would be Agnes Moorehead, Carol Burnett, Desi Arnaz, Dick Van Dyke, Elizabeth Montgomery, James Buchanan, Jerry Lewis, Joan

Rivers, Lucille Ball, Marion Lorne, Vivian Vance, William Frawley, and, of course, Harriet Lane. And I would ask America's First Lady to help me plan the entire evening!

Milton Stern
February 2005

Chapter 1
All Eyes Upon Her

On the evening of March 4, 1857, the invited guests, politicians, and Washington elite were gathered under the great tent, erected at Judiciary Square for the Inaugural Ball. The weather was perfect, and there was a large military presence to welcome the newly sworn-in chief executive. The crowd was milling about and alternating between dancing and enjoying the fine cuisine, which included 3,000 quarts of champagne, 400 gallons of oysters, 500 quarts of chicken salad, 500 quarts of jelly, 60 saddles of mutton, 16 sides of beef, 75 hams, and 125 beef tongues. It was all topped off with 1,200 quarts of ice cream. Three thousand dollars was spent on the wine alone.[1]

A few of the Washington society matrons, surprised at the extravagances, whispered behind their imported fans, but some of their peers informed them that fine dining and exquisite entertaining were to be expected from the new administration. The women were all too happy to see Jane Appleton Pierce return to New Hampshire as she had become known as the "Shadow in the White House." They were recalling how poor Mrs. Pierce had watched in horror as her son Benjamin was crushed in a train accident just weeks before her husband's inauguration. He was the last of her three children, and she blamed her husband's political ambitions for the deaths of all of them. Mrs. Pierce spent her four years in her rooms praying for her husband's soul, while he drank away his sorrows, much to the consternation of the *beau monde*, who were clamoring for any kind of White House entertaining. But that was not to be, for there were no receptions, luncheons or afternoon teas. These refined women were more than eager to dust off their seldom worn evening attire and fine bone corsets to return to a busy Washington social season.

At approximately 11:00 pm, the forty-piece orchestra playing under the swaying chandeliers struck up "Hail to the Chief." America's Bachelor President, James Buchanan, the fifteenth individual to hold the highest office in the land, made his entrance, escorted by a commission headed by Senator Albert J. Brown of Mississippi and Assistant Secretary of State John Appleton. He wore a Lancaster suit of black satin lined with the coat of arms of the then 31 states. While most eyes were on the tall, heavy-set, white-haired, 65-year-old President, they were quickly averted as they noticed the strikingly beautiful figure behind him. Robert, the chief usher, announced her name, and the guests parted like the Red Sea as the President's unmarried, 26-year-old niece made her Washington society debut.

Wearing a dress of white satin and lavender tulle that rivaled the latest fashions from Paris, with her hair adorned with lavender silk flowers that cascaded to the bodice of her gown, she was truly a sight to behold. She floated into the room and commanded the attention of the gentlemen and even the ladies. Exuding the style, flare and grace of a woman twice her years, she instantly established herself as their "Democratic Queen." The royalty that the founding fathers had so adamantly rejected had finally conquered the capital. All eyes were upon her beautiful, smiling face and exquisite gown, but they were soon averted by something even more breathtaking. A few jaws dropped as the guests soon found themselves staring at her décolletage, for the young hostess instructed her seamstress to lower the neckline on her inaugural gown an unheard of two and half inches. Her voluptuous endowment was presented for the world to admire. The men stood taller, and all the women, with the exception of the hostess herself, blushed with embarrassment for Washington society's newest arrival. How scandalous!

Fans were raised as the women covered their busy mouths, whispering and pointing. But when the earth refused to open up and swallow the offending bosom, the women realized they were witnessing something even more astonishing. For the first time in their young country's history, the White House had a hostess who was a fashion leader, establishing a style all her own.

The next day and over the course of the next few weeks, as stories and pictures of the Inaugural Ball appeared on the front pages of every major newspaper, there was not an idle dressmaker in Washington, or the rest of the country. Women from Maine to Florida, Pennsylvania to the Oregon Territory, instructed that the necklines be lowered on their own dresses to imitate the style of the most admired and beloved woman in the country, America's First Lady, Harriet Lane.

Chapter 2
Her Bachelor Uncle

As 11-year-old Harriet watched her make up the bed in the guest room, she asked, "Miss Hetty, how may guests are coming?" Her uncle's loyal housekeeper informed her that there would be three guests, along with the Senator's servant, John Bell. As they made their way down the stairs of the townhouse, the ever-inquisitive young lady wanted to know where everyone would sleep because her bed could sleep one, yet the guest room could sleep two. Miss Hetty replied that the Senator's sister, Margaret, would sleep in Harriet's room, and she would share the bed in the guest room with Catherine, his niece. The young lady continued to skip through the house, two steps behind Miss Hetty. The poor woman never imagined herself caring for a young child as she had assumed being employed by the 50-year-old bachelor meant there would be no children underfoot, which when she accepted the position suited her just fine.

"But Miss Hetty, where will the Senator sleep?" Harriet asked. Miss Hetty stopped, turned around, looked down at the young lady and said, "He will sleep with your uncle. Now don't you have anything better to do than to ask me questions?" Harriet's eyes grew wide as she saw her uncle standing behind Miss Hetty.

"Harriet, Miss Hetty has a lot of work to do, so unless you intend to be a help rather than a hindrance, may I suggest you quit asking her questions and go outside and play," her uncle told her. Harriet knew when to stop, and she turned around and skipped down the hallway exiting through the front door.

Only a few minutes had passed, when she saw the carriage pull up in front of their home. The driver was sitting next to a well-dressed black man. "Could that be John Bell?" she thought. But he was dressed like a butler and did not look like any of the slaves she saw depicted in the abolitionist pamphlets she had secretly read while away at school. The black man alighted from the carriage and assisted the two young women as they stepped down. Her uncle came out the front door and quickly made his way to the curb to welcome his invited guests. He introduced Harriet to Catherine and Margaret, but she was preoccupied with the black man who was assisting the Senator from the carriage. Senator Buchanan took his dear old friend by the arm and presented Harriet.

"This is my adopted daughter, Harriet Lane," Buchanan told his guest. "Harriet this is your uncle's dearest friend, Senator William Rufus Devane King of Alabama."

The Southern gentleman bowed and said, "My aren't you a pretty young lady. I know your uncle is very proud of you."

Harriet curtsied for Senator King, and then she pointed at John Bell and asked, "Is he a slave?"

Death was no stranger to American families in the 1800s. An individual was considered to have lived a full life upon reaching the ripe old age of 55. It was not unusual for children to die in infancy, for mothers to die during childbirth, or for an adult to die from a common infection that today would be treated with antibiotics. For the Buchanan family, death played a recurring and major role in shaping their lives and destinies. The paradox in Harriet Lane's life was that death enabled her to thrive and establish her place in the world often filling the void left by the departed. What would have broken weaker souls, only strengthened hers as she moved forward and remained an optimistic and prominent force in America's political and social arenas. It was a tragic death that occurred before Lane was born that enabled her to rise to positions in high society abroad and in

America. And, it was the tragic death of another powerful political figure that would enable her to become her uncle's closest confidante.

In 1791, the United States Constitution was four years old, and George Washington had served as President for two years. On April 23, James and Elizabeth Speer Buchanan welcomed their second child, James, into the world in a log cabin in "picturesque" Stony Batter, near Mercersberg, Pennsylvania. The senior Buchanan was born in Ireland and was an early pioneer of what was then considered Western Pennsylvania. He became a successful storekeeper and businessman, who provided well for his family. Elizabeth Speer was the daughter of a "respectable" farmer in Adams County, Pennsylvania, and she was known for her gift of "superior intellect" and her "earnest piety." She bore eleven children:[2]

> Mary Buchanan (1789) who died as an infant
> James Buchanan (1791) who never married (Fifteenth President
>   of the United States)
> Jane Buchanan (1793) who married Elliot Lane
>   (Harriet Lane's parents)
> Maria Buchanan (1795) who married four times: Jesse Magaw,
>   Thomas Johnson, Charles Yates, and Jacob Fronk
> Sarah Buchanan (1798) who married James Johnston Houston
> Elizabeth Buchanan (1800) who married Hugh Ferguson
> Harriet Buchanan (1802) who married Robert Henry
> John Buchanan (1804) who never married
> William Speer Buchanan (1805) who never married
> George Washington Buchanan (1811) who never married
> Edward Young Buchanan (1811) who married Ann Foster.
>   Edward was a Presbyterian minister and the only male
>   Buchanan to father children with his wife giving birth to
>   eleven. His oldest son, James, served as President James
>   Buchanan's private secretary.

In 1798, the Buchanan family moved to Mercersburg, located in Franklin County, which is southwest of Chambersburg between McConnellsburg and Greencastle near the Tuscarora Trail and the Maryland state line. In Mercersburg, seven-year-old James Buchanan began his formal education in English, Latin and Greek. James's left eye, in which he was farsighted, was set high in the socket, and he was nearsighted in his right eye. As a result, he closed his left eye and tilted his head when conversing with others. He was almost always photographed on the right side. A few of his political colleagues would later find his blinking distracting, referring to it as his "nervous twitching," and during his presidential campaign, an issue would be made of his "tilted head." Though his vision was impaired, he inherited his mother's intelligence and was accepted to and entered Dickinson College as a junior at the age of 16 in 1807.

Chartered in 1783, Dickinson College was the first college established in the newly recognized United States. The college was named after John Dickinson, the Penman and a signer of the Constitution. Typical of colleges at that time, Dickinson offered a liberal arts education with its campus located in Carlisle, Pennsylvania, a pre-Revolutionary War town.

Today, Dickinson ranks eighteenth in illustrious alumni.[3] Among them was 1795 Dickinson graduate and class valedictorian Roger Brooke Taney. Taney later served as Chief Justice of the United States, administering the presidential oath of office to James Buchanan and authoring a decision that would cast a shadow on his presidency.

Although young Buchanan excelled in his studies at Dickinson, one incident had a detrimental impact on his time there. According to the college archives, Buchanan found the school to be in "wretched condition" with "no efficient discipline." In the fall of 1808, he was expelled for "bad behavior."[4] There is no documentation of the exact cause of his expulsion because the academic records of Dickinson College were destroyed in a fire in 1904. Buchanan then made a pledge of good behavior to his minister, Dr. John King, a college trustee, and was readmitted to Dickinson the following term, graduating in 1809. According to the Dickinson Archives, "In his senior year, he felt slighted by the faculty because he did not win the top award of the College for which the literary society had nominated him. Buchanan commented, 'I left college, … feeling little attachment to the Alma Mater.'"[5] Still, his time spent at Dickinson would later come back to haunt him.

Buchanan went on to study law with Judge James Hopkins in Lancaster. At the time, Lancaster was the capital of Pennsylvania and the perfect location for a successful career as an attorney. He was admitted to the Pennsylvania Bar on November 12, 1812, and quickly gained an extraordinary reputation rarely seen among attorneys of his age and experience.

Also of note was Buchanan's military service during the War of 1812. In 1814, just before the British torched Washington, Buchanan addressed a public meeting in Lancaster, appealing to his fellow citizens' patriotism to "expel the intruders from a soil made sacred by the blood of their forefathers."[6] To prove his sincerity, Buchanan was the first to sign an open list for volunteers and thus entered the war as a private in the Pennsylvania State Militia in defense of Baltimore. Buchanan served under the command of Judge Henry Shippen. They marched to Baltimore, which was under threat of attack, and served under Major Charles Sterret Ridgely. Having defended Fort McHenry in Baltimore successfully in less than a month, the soldiers were honorably discharged in September 1814.[7] It was the day after the defense of Fort McHenry ended that Francis Scott Key wrote the "Star Spangled Banner," while a prisoner-of-war on a ship in Baltimore Harbor.

In 1814, with his military experience under his belt and as a member of the Federalist Party, Buchanan was elected as a Pennsylvania state assemblyman from Lancaster. Within a month of being elected to the State Assembly, Buchanan gave his ardent support to a bill appropriating $300,000 as a loan to the federal government to pay state volunteers and militias for service to the United States. It was the beginning of Buchanan's lifelong support for a strong military.

After two one-year terms as an assemblyman, Buchanan returned to his private practice in 1816, at the age of 25. He was then hired as the sole defense attorney in the impeachment trial of Judge James Walter Franklin, arguing his case before the Pennsylvania State Senate. Buchanan won the case, and his practice and reputation flourished as a result. Buchanan continued his law practice in Lancaster, and with a diligent work ethic and deft skills as a lawyer, he was soon earning more than $8,000 a year, quite a large sum in the early 1800s. Buchanan's success was reflected in his personal wealth as well, which was estimated to be valued at over $250,000 before his 30th birthday.

The future of Buchanan's professional life looked bright in the fall of 1818 when the 28-year-old jurist asked Ann Caroline Coleman to marry him. The dark-haired, 22-year-old Ann had been introduced to Buchanan by her cousin Eliza Jacobs, who was at the time being courted by Buchanan's colleague Molton Rogers. In the fall of 1819, Buchanan asked for her hand in marriage.

Ann's father happened to be Robert Coleman, a local businessman, who in 1802 had become a trustee of Dickinson College. He was a wealthy man who earned his fortune in the lucrative eighteenth century iron industry, and his business acumen and ambition earned him the distinction of being Pennsylvania's first millionaire.[8]

There are conflicting stories about the eventual break-up of Ann and Buchanan. In one version, Coleman, fearing that anyone who courted his daughter might have less than honorable intentions, used his connections with the college to gather whatever information he could about James Buchanan and his 1808 expulsion from Dickinson. Whatever information he obtained was damaging enough to instigate an argument between Ann and Buchanan that resulted in her breaking off the engagement.

Years later, Horatio King, who served as Buchanan's Postmaster General, told a different version to General Isaac R. Sherwood, an Ohio Democratic Congressman and lifelong Buchanan defender. The version was published in *The Washington Post*, on April 12, 1914.[9] A while after the engagement, Buchanan was "obliged to go out of town for a business trip." He returned after a few weeks and paid a visit to Horatio King's aunt, Mrs. William Jenkins, with whose husband he had an "intimate friendship." Her sister, Miss Gracie Hubley, also a daughter of General Hubley, a Revolutionary War officer, was staying at their home at the time. A "gossipy young lady told Miss Coleman of the visit," inciting jealousy in his fiancé. She was upset because on his way home he visited someone else before visiting her. As such, she penned an angry letter to him, releasing him from the engagement.

The story continues that the missive was handed to Buchanan while he was in the courthouse. "Persons who saw him receive it remarked that they noticed him turning pale when he read it."[10]

In both versions, Ann left a few days later with "an opera party" to Philadelphia. On December 9, 1819, Ann Caroline Coleman was found dead in a Philadelphia hotel. It was publicly stated that she died from "hysterics," but many believed that she committed suicide with an overdose of laudanum (a tincture of opium), which was a commonly prescribed barbiturate at the time. According to Horatio King, a poem, written by Buchanan and given to Ann after the break-up, was found on "her person" at the time of her death. Whatever the truth of what happened between Buchanan and Ann prior to her death, her family barred Buchanan from the funeral and from having any further contact with the Colemans.

In a desperate attempt to gain access to Ann's funeral, Buchanan drafted a letter on December 10, 1819, one day after her death. The letter, addressed to her father, was never sent, but it offers clues as to what led to the argument that might have caused the young woman to take her own life:

> You have lost a child, a dear dear child. I lost the only earthly object of my affections without whom life now presents to me a dreary blank. My prospects are all cut off. I feel that my happiness will be buried with her in the grave. It is now no time for explanation but the time will come when you will discover that she as well as I have been much much abused. God forgive the authors of it. My feelings of resentment against them whoever they may be are buried in the dust.
>
> I have now one request to make "for the love of God" of your dear departed daughter whom I loved ultimately more than any human being could love, deny me not. Afford me the melancholy pleasure of seeing her body before its internment. I would not for the world be denied this request.
>
> I must make another but from the misrepresentations which must have been made to you I am almost afraid. I would like to follow the remains to the grave as a mourner. I would like to convince the world — I hope yet to convince you that she was infinitely dearer to me than life. I may sustain the shock of her death — but I feel that happiness

> has fled from me forever. The prayer which I make to God without ceasing in that I yet may be able to show my veneration for the memory of my dear departed saint be my love subject — attachment to her surviving friend.
>
> May Heaven bless you — enable you to bear the shock with the fortitude of a Christian. I am forever your sincere grateful friend.[11]

James Buchanan would never ask for another women's hand in marriage, and from that point forward, he was a confirmed bachelor.

In 1825, in a strange twist to the Coleman legacy, Ann's sister Sarah committed suicide in Philadelphia when her brother Edward refused to let her marry William Augustus Muhlenberg, co-rector of St. James Episcopal Church in Lancaster. Today, both Coleman sisters would probably be diagnosed with clinical depression.

In order to aid James Buchanan's escape from the Ann Caroline Coleman controversy, his friends nominated him for Congress in 1820, and he was elected to the first of his five consecutive terms in the House of Representatives, serving from 1821–1831. Ann's possible suicide was not discussed during Buchanan's campaigns at that time. It would not surface again until he ran for president 36 years later as a defense of his bachelorhood.

In 1824, the disputed presidential election was thrown into the House of Representatives and John Quincy Adams was elected through what was described as the "Corrupt Bargain." Ironically, the "bargain" would prove both fateful and fruitful to Buchanan. In the election of 1824, Andrew Jackson had received the most popular and electoral votes, but there was no constitutionally mandated majority of electoral votes among the top three candidates who were members of the same political party. One of the candidates was Henry Clay, who threw his support to Adams in February 1825, after secret conferences between the two. As a result, Adams was elected on the first ballot. The supporters of Jackson declared this a "corrupt bargain," saying that Clay had put Adams into the White House in order to become his Secretary of State and successor. Many historians believe there was a bargain but no corruption. Of the

48 Senators, 13 voted against Henry Clay's confirmation as Secretary of State — the most that would vote against the confirmation of a Secretary of State. (On January 19, 2005, 13 Senators voted against the confirmation of Condoleeza Rice, earning her a second place position in this distinguished category. Henry Kissinger comes in a distant third with seven votes in 1973.)

Jackson believed that Buchanan, although one of his supporters, was involved in the "bargain," and upon his inauguration in 1831, he appointed Buchanan as Minister to Russia from 1832–1833. Jackson felt this appointment would retain Buchanan as a supporter, but keep him out of domestic politics and as far away as possible. This would be the first attempt by a president to send Buchanan far away to protect his own political ambitions, and in each instance, Buchanan fared the better.

James Buchanan's diplomatic appointment as Minister to Russia proved instrumental in his political career helping him to rise through the ranks of his party. He negotiated the United States' first commercial treaty with the Russian Empire, a delicate feat and great accomplishment for the young diplomat.

After returning from his post in Russia, James Buchanan was elected Senator from Pennsylvania in 1834, fulfilling William Wilkins's unfinished term. He was reelected in 1836 and 1842. While in the Senate, he chaired the Committee on Abolition Petitions and the Committee on Foreign Relations. It was there that he met Senator William Rufus Devane King of Alabama.

William Rufus Devane King was James Buchanan's closest friend in Washington and believed by many to be Buchanan's lover. They roomed together at different times while serving in Congress and corresponded for more than 18 years. The scant, surviving documents showed the correspondence between the two of them was usually posted through official and diplomatic channels, and discretion was always incorporated so as not to arouse the suspicions of those around them.

William Rufus Devane King, America's only bachelor vice president and the only one from Alabama, was born April 7, 1786, near Newton Grove in Sampson County, North Carolina. Vice President King is sometimes confused with Senator William

Rufus King of New York, who was a signer of the Declaration of Independence and one of the United States' early ambassadors to Great Britain. This confusion with the first King explains the rumors that persist to this day of the latter King's wearing of ribbons, scarves and powdered wigs long after they were in fashion. Vice President King always wore the contemporary styles of the early- to mid-1800s, and he never wore a wig. There are unconfirmed rumors that President Andrew Jackson referred to him as "Senator Nancy" or "Miss Fancy Pants" and that President James Knox Polk called him "Mrs. Buchanan."

His father was William King, a plantation owner who served in the North Carolina legislature and a member of the North Carolina Constitutional Conventions of 1788 and 1789. His mother, Margaret Devane, was the granddaughter of a French Huguenot, who in 1735 had immigrated to Wilmington, North Carolina. King was educated at Grove Academy in Kenansville and graduated from the University of North Carolina in Chapel Hill in 1803, and from there, he studied law under Judge William Duffy. He also became a member of the Masonic Lodge, as were James Buchanan and several other presidents and vice presidents including President George Washington. He practiced law in Clinton and was appointed solicitor for the Wilmington Judicial District. In 1810, as a North Carolina Jeffersonian Democrat, King was elected to the first of his three terms in the House of Representatives. In 1816, at the age of 30, he entered the diplomatic corps, and served for two years as Secretary of the Legation in Naples, Italy, and as Minister to Russia.

Many American families settled in the new territories of Alabama and Mississippi from 1815–1830. King, along with his mother, grandmother, two brothers and five sisters moved to Dallas County and Morengo County in Alabama. He founded the town of Selma, Alabama, which was near his plantation called King's Bend, located just across the Alabama River. He later built a home called Chestnut Hill in the Pine Hills near Selma. At the time of his death, his estate consisted of several plantations and 159 slaves.

Elected as one of Alabama's first two senators in 1819, King served in the Senate from 1819 to 1844 and again from 1849 until 1853.

James Buchanan and King struck up a friendship that lasted for the better part of 18 years and may have ended in 1850. Although they are rumored to have roomed together for all of that time, the progression of their careers and the partial year sessions of the United States Senate would have precluded such an extended living arrangement. King spent two years as Minister to France followed by two years in Alabama before returning to the Senate in 1849. Buchanan served for four years as Secretary of State before returning to Wheatland, his estate in Lancaster, in 1849. At the most, they may have roomed together for part of the eight years from 1835-1843, but only when the Senate was in session. Also, it was not unusual for men to share a bed when rooming together in a boarding house in the mid-1800s. King and Buchanan frequently walked arm and arm along the streets of Washington, which was another common practice. However, their enduring friendship did earn them the nickname "Siamese Twins,"[12] a euphemism for homosexual couples.

Although Buchanan and King were prolific letter writers, few letters between the two men have survived the centuries. Most of Buchanan's personal correspondence was destroyed in a New York warehouse fire in the early 1900s.

On September 16, 1868, Catherine Ellis, King's niece and a lifelong friend of Harriet Lane's wrote:

> There was at King's Bend a large bundle of letters from Mr. Buchanan to my Uncle and I hope they may not have been destroyed in the raid which was made on the place ... and shall immediately write to Miss King upon the subject and I will have them forwarded to you ... Among the souvenirs I have two or three letters given to me by my cousin and belong to the package I have maintained. These I will send to you as I return to Ala. Thankful as I have been for Mr. Buchanan's friendship and regarding him with affection as I always did.[13]

Although Ellis refers to a large bundle of letters, only a few have survived. Catherine Ellis was also King's travel companion and confidante. She was one of two individuals, his sister Margaret being the other, who were trusted to read any letters between King and Buchanan.

President John Tyler appointed Senator William Rufus Devane King Minister to Paris in 1844, and he served two years from 1844 to 1846. A letter that was written upon King's arrival in Paris and continued over several days has been often referred to as several letters in an attempt to give the illusion of a frustrated lover waiting for word from his intended. Interestingly, King's letters to Buchanan were quite long reaching lengths five times that of any other correspondence to or from Buchanan.[14]

King and Buchanan were friends with a Mrs. Roosevelt, who was often mentioned in their letters. Mr. Roosevelt was obviously comfortable with his wife being friends with two prominent bachelors, as there was never a note of protest, and he too was counted among their friends.

With Polk's election to the presidency in November 1844, James Buchanan was sent a letter on February 17, 1845, one month before the inauguration, from President-elect James Knox Polk, tendering him the position of Secretary of State:

> In making up my Cabinet, I desire to solicit Gentlemen who agree with me in opinion and who will cordially co-operate with me in carrying out the principles and policy.
>
> In my official action I will myself take no part between gentlemen of the Democratic party who may become aspirants or candidates to succeed me in the Presidential office, and desire that no members of my Cabinet shall do so. —
>
> Should any member of my Cabinet become a candidate for the Presidency or Vice Presidency of the United States, it will be expected upon than happenings of such an event — that he will retire from the Cabinet.
>
> If Sir, you concur with me in these opinions and desires, I shall be pleased to have your assistance in my administration as a member of my Cabinet and now tender to you the office of Secretary of State, and invite you to take charge of that Department.[15]

Although a copy of Buchanan's response has not survived, Buchanan did accept the position and served out his entire term as Secretary of State (1845–1849). Polk insisted that no members remain in his cabinet once declared a candidate for president or vice-president, which is especially noteworthy concerning Buchanan, whose name was considered for the presidency, beginning in 1844. This would be the second time a sitting president would make an attempt to remove Buchanan from the spotlight, and again it would be a failure.

As Secretary of State, James Buchanan signed documents and treaties that increased the territories of the United States by 30 percent. His first task was facilitating the acquisition of Texas, which was admitted as a slave state in 1845 and resulted in "Polk's War," as then one-term Illinois Representative Abraham Lincoln referred to the Mexican War (1846-48). Buchanan brokered the Treaty of Guadalupe Hidalgo in 1848. Through the terms of the treaty, the Rio Grande became the official southern boundary of Texas, and for $15,000,000, the United States purchased from Mexico the territories that would become California, Nevada, Utah, most of New Mexico and Arizona, and parts of Colorado and Wyoming. In addition, Buchanan brokered the Oregon Treaty of 1846 with Great Britain, which resulted in the establishment of the northwestern boundary between Canada and the United States and the United States having a "legitimate" claim to the Oregon Territory, an area consisting partially of the future state of Washington. William Rufus Devane King was instrumental in the founding of the state of Washington, and King County, Washington, was posthumously named after him.

James Buchanan and William Rufus Devane King remained close until 1850, when the letter writing came to a halt. Buchanan had become a strong opponent of the Compromise of 1850, and King one of its most vocal supporters, having drafted a portion of the document. Although passed with the hopes of quieting the controversies, it did more to destroy the Union than any act before.

King served as President Pro-tem of the Senate under five vice presidents. When President Zachary Taylor died in July 1850, he became President of the Senate in place of former Vice President Millard Fillmore. The Twenty-fifth Amendment to the Constitution was not adopted until 1967, thereby leaving the vice presidency vacant whenever a president died or left office before the end of his term. King was a highly respected member of the Senate and considered their expert on the Senate's parliamentary rules. Senator Henry Clay once said of King, "He is as serious as an undertaker." King and Clay were also bitter enemies.

In 1852, the Democratic convention was held in Baltimore, where Lewis Cass, James Buchanan (for the third time), and Stephen A. Douglas (whom Buchanan disliked immensely) were all contenders for the nomination. On the 49th ballot, the Democrats nominated Franklin Pierce of New Hampshire as the "dark horse" candidate. To appease the Buchanan supporters, they nominated William Rufus Devane King as their vice presidential candidate on the first ballot even though at the time King was ill with tuberculosis. The Whig candidate was Winfield Scott, and John Parker was the candidate of the Free Soilers. Pierce won the election with 254 electoral votes, with the Whigs winning 42 and the Free Soilers none. With the election results in King's favor, he resigned as President Pro Tem of the Senate, and having never married became America's Bachelor Vice President.

Due to King's failing health, Congress passed a special act so that he could take the oath of office while seeking treatment for his tuberculosis in Cuba. He took the oath there on March 24, 1853, being the only vice president to take the oath of office on foreign soil. King did not have the chance to serve any part of his term. His illness grew worse, and he returned to King's Bend, where he died on April 18, 1853.

Before he died, James Buchanan sent a letter to King's office in Washington. King never saw the letter. Upon learning that King was too sick to return to Washington, Buchanan sent a subsequent letter to Margaret King, who was in Washington closing King's offices. In it he requested that the former letter be destroyed. She then sent the following reply on March 19, 1853, to Buchanan. In the letter she referred to her brother as Col. King:

> I must leave to "expresseno silence" our emotions of gratitude.
> The letter addressed to Mr. K. has been _disposed_ of according to your _directions_. So soon as an opportunity presents, I shall pay my respects to the gentleman you refer me to.

> The appeal you make must be gratified. Should it be
> refused, you may readily imagine the cause.[16]

More than any other correspondence, the few lines above may prove the depth of the King-Buchanan relationship. Buchanan apparently sent a letter to King asking that he be given the opportunity to visit him one last time. After a three-year lapse in correspondence, intentional or not, one can only speculate what the "destroyed" letter contained. Margaret, ever dutiful to her brother and Buchanan, destroyed the letter, and she offered to make an appeal on Buchanan's behalf. She alluded to Buchanan's knowledge that the appeal might not be granted and that Buchanan would not be ignorant of the cause.

She, Catherine Ellis, probably Mrs. Roosevelt, and maybe even Harriet Lane herself, were likely the only witnesses to the true nature of their relationship. The truth about whether King and Buchanan were lovers was eventually buried with all the parties involved. But the rumors would surface again in 1856 and survive to this day.

The following December, when Congress convened, the Senate chamber and the President of the Senate's chair were draped in black for thirty days as a sign of mourning, and a 70-page booklet containing the eulogies of his fellow Senators was published. King is still considered one of the great Senators in United States History.

King County, Washington, was named after him until February 24, 1986, when it was renamed after Martin Luther King, Jr., because the county felt it inappropriate to be named after a slave owner. One wonders what they think of their state being named after George Washington, also a slave owner?

In William R. King's last will and testament, he freed selected slaves by ensuring their "safe arrival" in Liberia, a free state, or the District of Columbia. John Bell was one of those slaves who was freed, and he, along with his family, emigrated to Liberia. King also directed the purchase of slaves from other individuals so they may be united with their families, while at the same time bequeathing most of his slaves to his relatives.

William Rufus Devane King, the only vice president from Alabama, was buried with his brother John in a mausoleum in

Live Oak Cemetery in Selma, Alabama. A bust of him is still on display in the United States Capitol.

With the death of King, Buchanan depended more on Harriet Lane for friendship and support.

Chapter 3
Pretty Little Mistress
of the House

Jane Buchanan Lane, favorite sister of James Buchanan, and her husband, Elliot Tole Lane, welcomed their youngest child, Harriet, into the world on May 9, 1830. Jane Buchanan Lane died in 1839, and Harriet along with her siblings James, Elliot, and Mary, were orphaned in 1841, when their father died. Mary was sent away to school in Virginia. At the time, her brothers were old enough to be on their own, but Harriet was 11 years old.

James Buchanan, a single successful politician was the natural choice to become her guardian. So young Harriet moved in with "Nunc," as she referred to her uncle, and she lived in his Lancaster townhouse. Ironically, Robert Coleman was the former owner of the home.

Harriet attended a boarding school in Lancaster run by "the Miss Crawfords," but she was not happy there, and the next year, Buchanan sent her to the same school Mary was attending in Charlestown, Virginia (present-day Charleston, West Virginia).

In a published article, an unidentified acquaintance of James Buchanan's recalled the following story about 11-year-old Harriet Lane, which was a first glimpse into the young girl's extreme generosity:

Her uncle with whom she lived, gave a grand dinner one day to some foreign friends, and as I knew them all too well, I was honored with an invitation. We were awaiting dinner as we chatted in the drawing room, and I was wondering [why] the pretty little mistress of the house failed to appear. Miss Harriet's uncle was very proud of her. I heard him remark ... "I wish you to meet my little adopted daughter. She is quite remarkable."

Just then he had stepped to the window, as if looking for her. Suddenly turning, he said, "Excuse me a moment. I will return soon." He hurried out a side door to the piazza.

I followed him. He hastily called the cook, the butler, and the coachman and returned to the house flushed, excited, angry, [and] leaving me to settle the trouble.

In time, Miss Harriet entered the drawing room dressed in a charming gown of pale blue, her bonny hair fastened with ribbons like the sky, her violet eyes deep and dark like a pansy, her fair cheeks blushing. She was quite the mistress of the home, and ready to be presented to her uncle's stately guests. Everybody was delighted with Miss Harriet "And have you enjoyed this lovely day?" asked one of the distinguished men. "Oh, very much indeed thank you." But catching her uncle's eye, she blushed down to her throat.

Now this is what Mr. Buchanan and I had seen before dinner. Down the main street of Lancaster, Miss Harriet trundling a wheelbarrow full of wood! Her hat was hanging on one side of her head, her face was scarlet as a poppy, her young arms were braced strong and straight, her bare hands grasping the handles of the wheelbarrow like those of a peasant girl of Italy!

When the guests had departed, and we three, Mr. Buchanan, his niece and I, were sitting before the open fireplace, late that night, the courtly old gentleman asked in a despairing sort of tone, "Harriet what were you doing when I saw you?" "Why Uncle James, I was on my way to old black Tabitha's with a load of wood because it was growing cold so fast. She had not a stick."

...

Later in life, I saw her — a beautiful bride, but she was a thousand times handsomer that breezy afternoon, wheeling the wood to Tabitha.[17]

In February 1842, Buchanan wrote to Harriet:

There is no wish nearer my heart that you should become an amiable & intelligent woman; and I am rejoiced to learn that you shall continue at the head of your class. You can render yourself very dear to me by your conduct; and I anticipate with pleasure the months which I trust in heaven we may pass together after the adjournment of Congress.[18]

At the age of 16, Harriet Lane enrolled in Georgetown Visitation Convent, a Catholic School in Washington, D.C., a considerably unusual decision for a Presbyterian. But the school had an excellent reputation, and Harriet graduated with honors in 1849.

In 1848, after serving for three of his four years as Secretary of State, Buchanan's supporters tried to secure him the nomination for the second time. But it was to no avail, as Louis Cass became the Democratic candidate and former President Martin Van Buren ran on the Free Soil ticket. Interestingly, Charles Adams, son of John Quincy Adams, was the vice presidential candidate on the Free Soil ticket. That November, Whig candidate, Zachary Taylor, was elected the twelfth President of the United States. He died on July 9, 1850, and Millard Fillmore, a former housemate of Buchanan's, became the second vice president to ascend to the presidency and the last Whig to serve as chief executive.

With the Democratic Party out of power, James Buchanan retired to Wheatland, his newly purchased estate in Lancaster.

The Wheatland mansion was a classic example of the federal architecture of the time. William Jenkins of Lancaster built "The Wheatlands" as it was originally named in 1828 due to the surrounding wheat fields. Buchanan purchased the Wheatlands, the 22 acres of land surrounding it and the adjacent buildings (privies, stables and the like) for $6,750 in December 1848 from Philadelphia attorney William Morris Meredith. As the new gentleman of the manor, Buchanan changed the name to "Wheatland."[19] Buchanan described Wheatland as "a beau ideal of a statesman's abode." Wheatland was Buchanan's home for the remainder of his life. Naturally, Harriet moved in with him at Wheatland, and she was given the responsibility of decorating the home and purchasing the majority of the furniture — with his approval.

He would soon be exposed to the frustrations of homeownership and dealing with contractors, as he wrote to Harriet on October 12, 1850:

> Mr. McSwain of Philadelphia, with whom I had contracted to put up a furnace & kitchen range this week has disappointed me & I cannot leave home until this work shall be finished. He writes me that he will certainly commence on Monday morning; if it is so, I hope to be in New York the beginning of the week after, say bout the 22 Instant.[20]

Buchanan even had trouble purchasing a mechanical refrigerator, which at the time used a vapor compression cycle operated by a crank. On August 6, 1851, he wrote to a Mr. J. M. Smith:

> I regret very much that you did not receive my order for a Refrigerator. It was sent to you immediately after the publication of a sketch of your biography with the Atlas: and I presumed as the money was not forwarded for want of a knowledge of the price, that you might have been unwilling to forward the article to a stranger. The season is now considerably advanced, I can very well do with what I have until another year, especially as I shall be from home much of the time between this & October.[21]

Buchanan's housekeeper throughout this time was Miss Hetty, a formidable force, who did not get along swimmingly with her employer's favorite niece. In semi-retirement, Buchanan, when not overseeing work at his home, traveled extensively, often meeting with politicians to discuss his future ambitions, and frequently, he was hob-knobbing with the crowds in which the wealthy bachelor was accustomed. While vacationing in Saratoga Springs in August 1852, Buchanan wrote to Harriet:

> I find the Springs very agreeable & the company very pleasant; yet there does not appear to be so many of the "dashers" here as I have seen. The crowd is very great in fact it is quite a mob of fashionable folks. Mrs. Plitt is very agreeable & quite popular. Mrs. Slidell is the most gay,

brilliant, & fashionable lady at the Springs; as I am her
admirer & attached to her party I am thus rendered a little
more conspicuous in the beau monde than I could desire.
Mrs. Rush conducts herself very much like a lady & is quite
popular. She has invited me to accompany her to Albini's
concert tomorrow evening, I would rather go with her to any
other place. Albini is the rage here.[22]

Fortunately, for both of them, Buchanan's social circle was
soon to go beyond the Saratoga Springs to a far off land that the
young Harriet Lane always dreamed of visiting. However, it
would take quite a bit of cajoling from the young lady to get her
overly protective uncle to invite her along for the ride.

Chapter 4
A Jolly Good Appointment

The newly confirmed Minister to the Court of St. James sat across from the President's desk and looked around the room, wondering if some day, he would occupy this space in the White House. President Pierce entered the room apologizing for his tardiness, and James Buchanan stood and assured the new President that all was forgiven. The gentlemen shook hands, and Buchanan was surprised to smell liquor on the chief executive's breath so early in the day. Perhaps the rumors were true.

The President sat first and Buchanan followed suit. There was the usual exchange of pleasantries before Pierce outlined his views on the elder statesman's new appointment. Buchanan listened and nodded, while thinking, "How did this man ever get elected?"

Pierce concluded their conversation with talk of entertaining other dignitaries while serving in the mission. He made suggestions about protocol and expenses, and then he leaned toward Buchanan.

"As a bachelor, I think it would behoove you to assign an experienced woman to act as your official hostess rather than solely take on the duties of entertaining your guests," the President said.

Pierce continued, "There are a few ... shall we say ... mature widows around town that would be more than happy to accompany you and act in that capacity."

James Buchanan smiled at the President and said, "You have nothing to worry about Mr. President. I have the perfect young woman in mind."

At the age of 61, James Buchanan considered his chances at ever being elected to the highest office in the land quite dim when Franklin Pierce was elected the fourteenth President of the United States in November 1852. However, Buchanan might have been the only member of his political party to feel that way. Considering the old statesman to be a prominent force in the Democratic Party, the newly elected President followed the lead of two of his predecessors, Jackson and Polk. He sent Buchanan as far away as possible by tendering his name for Minister to the Court of St. James in England.

Buchanan was rumored to be on the short list for the ambassadorship, but the ever-cautious statesman would not speak of its possibility until he actually received word from the President. Harriet wanted very much for her uncle to be offered and accept the appointment as she loved to travel and considered England a fascinating place to spend four years. However, he worried about where to send her if he went and at the time was not considering the idea of inviting her to accompany him. In a letter to Harriet, written 11 days after Pierce's inauguration, he wrote:

> You ask: Will you accept the mission to England? I answer, that it has not been offered, I have not the least reason to believe from any authoritive [sic] source that it will be offered. Indeed, I am almost certain that it will not because surely General Pierce would not nominate one to the Senate without first asking one whether I would accept. Shall the offer be made, I know not what I might conclude. Personally, I have not the least desire to go abroad as a foreign minister. But "sufficient unto the day is the evil thereof." I really would not know where to leave you, were I to accept a foreign mission, & this would be one serious objection.[23]

Buchanan was known to open Harriet's mail and read it before forwarding it to her, even when they were residing together. In a letter dated March 19, 1853, he had opened a letter from a Mr. Crosby, and unashamedly offered Harriet his advice on a reply. In the same letter, he addressed the possibility of the mission to England and how it would "spoil" his young niece:

> I think that a visit to Europe, with me as minister would spoil you outright. Besides it would consume your little independence. One grave objection to my acceptance of the mission, for whether I have no personal inclination, would be your situation. I should dislike to leave you behind in the care of any person I know.[24]

Again, he worried about the consequences of taking Harriet to England with him and about where to send her. Although she was 22 years old, in 1853 a single woman her age would either be married or left to live out her days with relatives as a spinster, but she would never live alone. Buchanan was offered the mission, and he wrote to Harriet while in transit to Washington on April 7:

> I am thus far on my way to Washington, wholly uncertain whether I shall accept or decline the mission. This will depend upon circumstances, which I cannot know until after my arrival in the city. I have not the least personal inclination to go abroad. Your letter was highly gratifying to me. As soon as I shall have decided, I will inform you of it.[25]

James Buchanan did accept the position and served as the Minister to the Court of St. James from 1853 to 1856. President Pierce advised Buchanan that as a bachelor it would behoove him to appoint a lady to serve as his hostess, and Buchanan tendered his favorite niece the position. Before he sailed by steamer, he wrote a letter dated August 4, 1853, from the Astor House in New York. In it he pushed for his niece to consider seeing John Van Buren, son of former President Martin Van Buren. He also spoke of her impending arrival in London, as Harriet Lane had eagerly accepted the unpaid job:

> John Van Buren called to see me this morning & was
> particularly amiable. He talked much of what his father had
> written & said to him respecting yourself, expressed great
> desire to see you, we talked much about you. He intimated
> that his father had aroused him to address you. I told him he
> would make for me a very rebellious nephew & would be
> hard to manage.
>
> He asked where you would be this winter. I told him you
> would be visiting your relatives in Virginia in the frame of a
> month & might probably come to London next Spring or
> Summer.[26]

This appointment would prove most fortuitous to both Buchanan and Harriet, who joined him in England for 18 months from the spring of 1854 to the fall of 1855. Buchanan wrote her the following upon his arrival:

> On the day before yesterday I received your kind letter of
> the 28 August with a letter from Mary which I have already
> considered. How rejoiced I am that she is content & happy
> in San Francisco. I also received your favor of the 18 August
> in due time. I write you this evening because I have
> important dispatches to prepare for the Department
> tomorrow to be sent by Saturday's steamer.
>
> How rejoiced I am that you did not come with me!
> Perceiving your anxiety, I was several times on the point of
> saying to you come along; but you would see as much
> fashionable society at Wheatland as you would see here
> until February or March next. You cannot conceive how dull
> it is; although personally I am content. The beau monde are
> all at their country seats or on the Continent there to remain
> until the meeting of Parliament.[27]

Had Buchanan not accepted the appointment, he would have remained in retirement and been relegated to historical obscurity, and few would have known about Harriet Lane. In England, Harriet blossomed and became a fixture in the prominent social circles that included the royal family, as she dined frequently with her uncle, Queen Victoria and Prince Albert. She developed a friendship with the royal family that served her well as Buchanan's official hostess in London. Queen Victoria was so pleased and impressed with Harriet Lane that she granted her the status of a diplomat's spouse and gave her the title "Honorary Ambassadress." Harriet thus became one of the first ladies of the diplomatic corps at St. James.

On a visit to Paris, she was called the "Girl Queen," and when Lord Tennyson and Buchanan received the degree of Doctor of Civil Laws at the same time at the University of Oxford, the students cheered her en masse.[28]

Upon her arrival in London in May 1854, Harriet wrote the following to one of her dearest friends, Lily Macalester:

> Though, as yet I have not much of interest to relate, concerning myself. — I only arrived here on Saturday evening and until presented to the Queen, will not be fairly in the "London world" ... My court-dress is now absorbing most of my attention, as I will be presented this day week (11th) ... I go to decide upon it today. Last evening we went to a Literary Club dinner — the ladies of course in the gallery. I was disappointed in the speaking — we had expected several distinguished speakers but only heard Lord Mahon, & Lord Stanley both men of talent. — Lord Mahon was the best speaker at the table — but he talked too much, and said too little. Lord Stanly talked a great deal, and said nothing. I was gratified to see the manner of conducting a public dinner here, but without doubt, our people are more prompt and eloquent — in fact, I have seen no improvements upon our country, except in servants, — here they are most respectful and respectable. ... Tomorrow and Saturday I go to dinner parties, and I suppose will be fairly launched in the gay world, after next week. ... I was charmed at the Opera last night. Beethoven's Fidelio was the piece. I heard the great Cravelli, and think her superb — the music is grand & effective. Mr. Peabody's box is opposite the Queen's — she, Prince Albert, & two of the children were there. Mr. P. is very kind — he had a large party of Americans last evening — and seems ready to entertain any who come ...
>
> Capt. West is a glorious fellow — I [never met] a more agreeable escort.[29]

While in Europe, the young and beautiful Harriet Lane was pursued by numerous suitors. She received two marriage proposals, one from Sir Fitz-Roy Kelly, a wealthy 59-year-old, and by 30-year-old Job Tyson, who traveled to England just to court her, only to be rejected in London and later back in the

United States.[30] Harriet's aplomb in being in the company of the royal family and London high society proved to "Nunc" that she was a most agreeable and admirable representative of the United States.

Shortly after her return to the United States, Harriet Lane's only sister, Mary, died suddenly in the fall of 1855, while living with her family in San Francisco. Harriet threatened to join a convent and retreated from society while grieving her sister. However, the political events of the following year presented an opportunity that she could not resist.

Chapter 5
Buchanan's Last Campaign

Late into the night on November 4, 1856, Harriet Lane sat with her uncle and the throng of supporters in the parlor at Wheatland awaiting the results of the election. She tried to busy herself with her embroidery, but it did little to calm her nerves. Since approximately 7:00 pm, a courier would arrive every so often from the telegraph office with the latest results. With each report, the supporters, who considered themselves experts in electoral politics, made their predictions. The only calm individual in the room was her uncle.

Harriet watched "Nunc" and admired his ability to control his emotions. She attributed his demeanor to his 40-year career in public service and the fact that he had never lost an election.

She tried to thread another needle, but her hands were shaking too much. She stood and announced that she was going into the kitchen and asked if anyone desired a snack. But the gentlemen were too busy bending her uncle's ear with their views.

As she stood in the kitchen, she saw what looked like a few people holding torches and walking down the road. She stared for a few minutes hoping to get a better view, and then she realized what was happening. Harriet watched as the mob of hundreds made their way up the drive and stood at the door cheering and calling for her uncle. She found herself unable to move. She then heard the gentlemen cheering in the parlor as they opened the front door. Her uncle, President-elect James Buchanan, stepped out onto the porch and thanked his supporters and the citizens of the great state of Pennsylvania.

Harriet Lane beamed with pride as she watched her uncle finally achieve his dream, and she thought, "What am I going to wear to the inauguration?"

After two failed attempts by his supporters to gain him the nomination, all Buchanan had ever needed was to leave the country. Ironically, Jackson, then Polk, and finally Pierce had pushed Buchanan closer to the top, while trying to remove him from the spotlight. Buchanan's service in England for the four years prior to 1856 was exactly what he needed to become a viable candidate, as he was the only presidential hopeful not caught up in the domestic mess that was evolving in the United States.

The Whig party, whose last successful presidential candidate was Zachary Taylor, was a victim of the slavery question and particularly, the Kansas-Nebraska Act. This resulted in one of the most violent episodes in American history as anti- and pro-slavery factions converged on the beleaguered territories. The Whigs held a fruitless convention where only Northern states and a few border slave states sent delegates. They stuck to their Whig roots and continued their tradition of nominating war heroes, albeit a minor one named William Drayton. Curiously the runner-up for their vice presidential nomination was Abraham Lincoln.

Millard Fillmore was the second vice president to ascend to the presidency, following the death of Zachary Taylor, thus making him the thirteenth president. Fillmore was the nominee of the American party, which was the extreme Northern wing of what was once the Whig Party. The cause of the rift was that many thought the party platform was too weak on its objection to the spread of slavery. His vice presidential running mate was Andres J. Donelson, a nephew of Andrew Jackson and the editor of *The Washington Union*. The party was also called the Know-Nothings and was extreme in its views toward immigrants, Catholics and minorities in general.

With the demise of the two-party system that for more than twenty years dominated the landscape of American politics, numerous northern Democrats left their party and joined the "anti-slavery Whigs" to found the new Republican Party. That party's platform was organized around a desire for the West to be without the "peculiar institution." Abraham Lincoln was among those who eventually joined the Republicans. The Republicans' first candidate for president was Major John C. Frémont (1813–1890), who was popular for his mapmaking expeditions to the West.

But Frémont was not without controversy. He was court-martialed, on the grounds of mutiny and disobeying orders, on January 31, 1848. General Stephen Kearny brought charges against Frémont regarding who held the governing authority in California. Mexico had ceded the territory to the United States in accordance with the Treaty of Guadalupe Hidalgo. During the Mexican War, Frémont was appointed military governor of California by Commodore Robert F. Stockton in 1847. At the same time, federal authorities sent Kearny to California to establish a government. Not surprisingly, tensions developed between the two men and in August 1847, Kearny ordered Frémont arrested and charged with insubordination. Frémont was eventually found guilty by a court-martial and included in his punishment was his removal from the army. President Polk reversed the decision, but Frémont resigned his commission anyway. The controversy did not affect his popularity, and he and his wife Jesse Benton Frémont, daughter of Missouri Senator Thomas Hart Benton, continued to reside at their Mariposa County, California, estate. Frémont became a multimillionaire during the gold rush, and he was elected as one of California's first senators in 1850. In 1855, the Frémonts moved to New York, where he earned a reputation as an out-spoken abolitionist and campaigned as the "Pathfinder" who would lead the country out of the shame of slavery.

The following are the lyrics of the Republican Party's campaign song:

> Journeyer in the distant mountains,
> O'er the land has spread thy fame,
> Hope is opening FREEDOM'S fountains,
> 'Neath the influence of thy name.
> Come and rescue Fair Columbia,

From her shame.
Raise on high fair Freedom's banner.
Ensign of the brave and true,
'Midst the din of party clamour,
Onward LEAD the battle through,
Never weary,
Till we've routed slavery's crew.

The aforementioned Kansas-Nebraska Act nearly ruined the careers of the two most prominent men who supported it — President Franklin Pierce and Senator Stephen Douglas. Douglas could have been the front-runner for the Democratic nomination in 1856, but he faced extreme opposition to the nomination from the Northern wing of the party. Pierce had significant support from the South and West, but was also fiercely opposed in the North. As a result, he became the seventh one-term president in a row, with Andrew Jackson's reelection win in 1832 being the last successful reelection bid until Abraham Lincoln would run for reelection in 1864.

James Buchanan, who had not been in the country for the prior four years and was therefore removed from the domestic controversies of the day, finally was in a position to obtain what he had hoped for as far back as 1844. Buchanan entered the convention in Cincinnati in July 1856 as the front-runner. Buchanan's record in Congress, his service in Russian and England, and his being a native of Pennsylvania — a populous free state — gave the Democrats what they did not think they had in 1856, a viable candidate. Pennsylvania was the first state to abolish slavery (March 1, 1780).

A little known fact is that Buchanan was personally opposed to slavery, and he would purchase slaves in order to grant them their freedom.

Buchanan, a believer in the strict interpretation of the Constitution, always insisted that slavery should be a matter for individual states and territories to decide. As such, he perpetuated what some who had framed the Constitution feared — that by not addressing the issue in 1787, it would eventually divide this "precious union." Buchanan's views, interpreted by many as pro-slavery, won him Southern support. To be clear, Buchanan was not pro-slavery, but he believed strongly in the rights of the individual states. He believed that if left alone, the South would abolish slavery in due time, but that the agitation of the abolitionists would only aid in the South's persistence to hold on to the institution. Always the diplomat, he would support any policy or compromise that would avoid war and "agitation."

"Before many years the abolitionists will bring war upon this land," Buchanan said, "It may come during the next presidential term."

In his memoirs, *Mr. Buchanan's Administration, on the Eve of Rebellion*, Buchanan stated his position on the abolitionists and the slaveholders clearly, and he also alluded to the framers of the Constitution who left the "question of slavery" to the individual states in order to secure the Union:[31]

> It is easy to imagine the effect of [the agitation of the abolitionists] upon the proud, sensitive and excitable people of the South. One extreme naturally begets another. Among the latter there sprung up a party as fanatical in advocating slavery as were the abolitionists of the North in denouncing it. At the first, and for a long time, this party was small in numbers, and found it difficult to excite the masses to support its extreme views. These Southern fanatics, instead of admitting slavery to be an evil in itself, pronounced it to be a great good. Instead of admitting that it had been reluctantly recognized by the Constitution as an overruling political necessity, they extolled it as the surest support of freedom among the white race. If the fanatics of the North denounced slavery as evil and only evil, and that continually, the fanatics of the South upheld it as fraught with blessings to the slave as well as to his master. Far different was the estimation in which it was held by Southern patriots and statesmen both before and for many years after the adoption of the Constitution. These looked forward hopefully to the day when, with safety both to the white and black race, it might be abolished by the people of the slaveholding States themselves, who alone possessed the power.
>
> [I] as Senator of the United States, from December 1834 until March 1845, lost no opportunity of warning [my] countrymen of the danger to the Union from a persistence in this anti-slavery agitation, and of beseeching them to

suffer the people of the South to manage their domestic affairs their own way. ...

Although, in Pennsylvania, we are all opposed to slavery in the abstract, yet we will never violate the Constitutional compact which we have made with our sister States. Their rights will be held sacred by us. Under the Constitution it is their own question, and there let it remain.

There was a popular belief by those who voted for Buchanan that his diplomatic skills would help the nation avert war. What Buchanan wanted twelve years earlier, he was hesitant about in 1856. But at 65 years of age, he also knew that if he were ever to be president, this was his last chance. At the convention, Buchanan was nominated on the seventeenth ballot with the required two-thirds majority, considered an easy victory in the nineteenth century, which was a far cry from today's conventions where the nominee is all but officially decided months beforehand. John Cabell Breckinridge of Kentucky was nominated as James Buchanan's running mate.

Breckinridge was the only vice president ever to take up arms against the government of the United States. Although his cousin was Mary Todd Lincoln and his home state of Kentucky remained in the Union, Breckinridge chose to volunteer his services to the Confederate Army. The United States Senate formally expelled him as a traitor. When the Confederates were defeated, Breckinridge's was forced into exile abroad, bringing a promising political career to an ignominious end.

Both Buchanan and Frémont conducted their campaigns in the tradition of the times, by not campaigning at all. They neither made public appearances, nor spoke to the press. Active campaigning was considered un-gentlemanly and almost un-American, as one should never seek power with the greed of an active campaigner. Buchanan left the campaigning to the "Buchaneers," as his supporters came to be known; and Frémont depended on many followers, among them Abraham Lincoln, to make speeches in support of his candidacy.

Although the campaigns were not conducted directly by the candidates, they were not short on mudslinging and dirty politics, perhaps even more so than modern campaigns for the presidency. Democrats created badges called "Black Republican," which depicted a runaway slave, and they also made issue of Frémont's out-of-wedlock birth. But even more controversial at the time was the rumor spread by the Democrats concerning Frémont's Catholic Church wedding. To have a Catholic president who was married in a church was more than nineteenth century voters could tolerate. But the Democrats were not alone in their mudslinging.

The Republicans nicknamed Buchanan "Ten-Cent Jimmy" after he publicly stated that he considered ten cents a day a fair wage for manual laborers. They also made an issue of his age, as he would be the second-oldest person elected president at the time if he won. However, it was the "whispering campaign" that would inflict the most damage. First was the rumor that Buchanan's tilting of his head while speaking to someone was not due to his eye condition but the result of a failed attempt to hang himself. And second, was the curiosity surrounding his bachelorhood as the past rumors of Buchanan and King having a homosexual relationship were resurrected in an effort to discredit him. Neither worked.

The November 1856 election results were:

Candidates	Party	Electoral Vote	Popular Vote
James Buchanan John C. Breckinridge	Democrat	174	1,832,955
John C. Frémont William L. Dayton	Republican	114	1,339,932
Millard Fillmore Andrew J. Donelson	Know Nothing	8	871,731

Although none of the candidates carried a popular majority, Buchanan carried enough states to win in the required Electoral College majority. Buchanan carried 19 states, mostly in the South: Alabama, Arkansas, California, Delaware, Florida, Georgia, Illinois, Indiana, Kentucky, Louisiana, Mississippi, Missouri, New Jersey, North Carolina, Pennsylvania, South Carolina, Tennessee, Texas, and Virginia. Frémont carried 11 states, mostly in the North: Connecticut, Iowa, Maine, Massachusetts, Michigan, New Hampshire, New York, Ohio, Rhode Island, Vermont, and Wisconsin. Fillmore carried one state: Maryland.

James Buchanan's win made him the first in two respects. He was the first and only president from Pennsylvanian. He was also the only bachelor to be elected president and remain a bachelor for the remainder of his term. Buchanan was the last Democrat to be elected president until Grover Cleveland was elected to his first term 28 years later in 1884. Cleveland was also a bachelor when elected, but in June 1886, the 49-year-old Cleveland married 22-year-old Frances Folsom, making him the first president to marry while in office. At 65, Buchanan was also our third oldest president-elect behind William Henry Harrison at age 67 (November 1840) and Ronald Reagan at 69 (November 1980). Buchanan was also the last person born in the eighteenth century to be elected president, making him the last Federalist Era President. Buchanan would also be the only President of the United States when the flag of the United States had 32 stars (representing the 32 states in the second year of his term (1858–59)). James Buchanan was also the last former Secretary of State to be elected president ending a long standing tradition of using that post as a stepping stone to the highest office in the land.

Whether first, only, or last, President James Buchanan's White House would have more style and elegance than anyone could recall thanks to his niece, Harriet Lane.

Chapter 6
Two Days of Bliss and
Four Years of Turmoil

On March 4, 1857, in what would be the first presidential inauguration to be photographed, James Buchanan took the oath of office on the east front of the United States Capitol and thus became the fifteenth President of the United States. In the tradition of the day, Buchanan gave his inaugural address before taking the oath of office. One of the surviving rumors about Buchanan concerning the Democratic Party's rejection of him in 1860, thus denying him the nomination and a possible second term, is unfounded. Buchanan stated in his inaugural address that he would not seek a second term, as his age was most probably a factor.

He also addressed the pending *Dred Scott* decision that the Supreme Court was expected to hand down within days. He called for a stronger military, especially the navy, which at the time he considered insufficient to protect our coasts. Contrary to modern thinking, the Congress in his time felt that in times of peace, a strong military gave too much power to the president and was therefore a dangerous proposition, which would invite war rather than prevent it. Buchanan would fight and lose the battle for a strong military his entire term in office.

Following his taking the oath of office, there was a parade down Pennsylvania Avenue, which held greater significant since Buchanan was the favorite son of that state. That evening, an inaugural ball was held in an enormous temporary structure, erected at Judiciary Square. Both were the first of their kind to be photographed and etchings of the photographs were printed on the front pages of newspapers, so the country could enjoy the inauguration through pictures as well as eyewitness accounts.

With the upbeat atmosphere of the inauguration, Americans were hopeful that their new president, a master of diplomacy and an experienced and respected public servant, would help to heal the wounds that threatened to tear the nation apart. Unfortunately, this mood lasted for just two days, for on March 6, 1857, the Supreme Court handed down the *Dred Scott* decision, the most controversial decision of the time, and a turning point in American history.

The two trials of Dred Scott were held in 1847 and 1850, and eventually worked their way up to the United States Supreme Court. Dred Scott was born into slavery in Virginia in 1799 and was the property of the Peter Blow family. Scott was a slave his entire life, and like most slaves, was illiterate. In 1830, the Blows moved to St. Louis, and they took their slaves with them. As they experienced financial difficulties, Dred Scott was sold to Dr. John Emerson, a military surgeon stationed at Jefferson Barracks. Scott accompanied Emerson to posts in Illinois and the Wisconsin Territory, where slavery had been prohibited by the Missouri Compromise of 1820. Dred Scott married fellow slave Harriet Robinson, at Fort Snelling, and they had two children, Eliza and Lizzie. Emerson married Irene Sanford, and the Emersons returned with their slaves to St. Louis in 1842, where Dr. Emerson died the following year. Irene Emerson hired out the entire Scott family to other families in order to pay her debts.

Dred and Harriet Scott filed a suit for their freedom on April 6, 1846, against Irene Emerson. The basis for the suit was the fact that for nine years, the Scotts lived in free territories with their owners but made no attempt to gain their freedom. Although no one is sure why he waited so long to file a suit, many believed that Scott heard a rumor that he was being sold, so the suit was not believed to be filed for political reasons. What was known was that the Missouri courts in the past supported the doctrine of "once free, always free." Scott did not have any money, but he found an ally in his original owners, the Blows, who provided the financial resources necessary to file the suit. It was with their support that the case was able to survive the many battles that ensued over the next eleven years.

As difficult as this is to fathom today, in 1846, what was important for the courts in this case was not the rights of the Scotts and their freedom, but the rights of property owners. And, if slaves were property, could they be separated from their owners simply because it was illegal to own such property in another state? The difference between slaves and other property was that slaves could sue, and this became the central issue of the case: Could slaves sue for their freedom?

Their first trial was lost because the evidence presented was hearsay. However, the judge granted them the right to a second trial. In 1850, a second trial was held, and the jury decided that the Scotts should be free. Emerson appealed her case to the Missouri State Supreme Court. In 1852, the ruling was reversed by the state supreme court, which based its ruling on the fact that Missouri law allowed for slavery and the slaves had no rights. In 1854, armed with a team of abolitionist lawyers, Scott filed suit in St. Louis Federal Court. The case was decided against Dred Scott, so he appealed to the U.S. Supreme Court.

Fellow Dickinson College Graduate, Chief Justice Roger B. Taney, delivered the majority opinion in the *Dred Scott* case. Although seven of the nine justices agreed that Scott should remain a slave, the Court went beyond the immediate case in its decision. The Court ruled that Dred Scott and all slaves were not citizens of the United States and therefore had no right to file suits in federal courts. The Court also declared that Scott had never been free because slaves were personal property. Therefore, the Missouri Compromise of 1820 was unconstitutional, meaning the federal government had no right to prohibit slavery in any of the new territories. Worse than any other result of the decision was that the Court gave federal authorities the right to enforce the dreaded fugitive slave laws, which dated back to 1793. Any slave who escaped to a free state was no longer free by virtue of stepping on free soil. As a result, the Underground Railroad expanded rapidly, and hundreds of slaves escaped to Canada, where slavery was illegal.

Any hopes Buchanan had of avoiding the slavery issue while president were soon dashed as a result of the *Dred Scott* decision, and the country would become more divided as Southern states declared victory, and many Northern states declared they would ignore the decision. Ignoring a Supreme Court decision would only weaken the federal government and divide the nation further. Buchanan, who believed strictly in his oath of office, chose to enforce the decision whether he supported it or not. The once-strong Democratic Party began to split in two. Ironically, Buchanan was led by an unreliable source to believe the *Dred Scott* decision would be decided in favor of the plaintiff, and he alluded to this fact in his inaugural address.

The expansion of slavery into new territories was enough to sour Buchanan's first days in office, and the Panic of 1857 made everything bitter. Up to that time, America was enjoying an economic boom, which had begun at the end of the Mexican War in 1848. On August 24, 1857, the *Central America,* a ship that was carrying 400 passengers and a shipment of 30,000 pounds of gold from the San Francisco Mint, was sailing into a hurricane, and U.S. banks were dependent on the shipment reaching its destination. The banks had invested in businesses that were failing, and a bank panic had resulted. Consequently, railroads were losing their ability to pay their debts, and investors were experiencing heavy losses in the stock market. In addition, speculators in land who had gambled on railroad construction were experiencing heavy losses.

In 1857, banks dealt in their own paper currency (a federal law prohibited the government from printing paper money), so they used silver and gold to back up their various currencies. When people panicked and withdrew their money, the banks needed the gold from the *Central America* and other sources to close out their accounts. The public's confidence in the government's ability to back the banks' paper currency with specie was waning.

The *Central America* sank, and a chain of events soon followed. The New York branch of the Ohio Life Insurance and Trust Company collapsed amidst a huge embezzlement scandal, and many banks across the country either failed or collapsed. British investors chose to remove funds from American banks. Grain prices fell, and the pileup of unsold manufactured goods led to large layoffs. More railroads failed, and the country was in a major economic depression. To avert more disaster, in October, a bank holiday was declared in New England and New York, so that further runs could not be made on institutions in those two states. The depression eventually spread to Europe, South America and the Far East. There was no significant recovery in the United States for 18 months, and the country would not recover fully until the Civil War when government contracts (and a growing black market for goods) would help investors in the North.

Ironically, the South was not severely affected by the Panic of 1857, which led many Southerners to come to the conclusion that the basis of their economy was far superior to that of the rest of the country.

And then there was Utah. Utah proved to be a nuisance during Buchanan's term. Territorial Governor Brigham Young defied the government at every opportunity and proved to be an unconstitutional authority as he was also head of the Mormon Church. His appointment and his conduct left him with no government in Utah except for himself, and thus Young became a dictator in the territory. Buchanan immediately appointed another territorial governor, who with the aid of the military was able to remove Young from power before he was able to stage a full out rebellion against the United States.

That was just the first year.

Buchanan's Cabinet from 1857 through the end of 1860 was:

Secretary of State Lewis Cass (1857–1860)
Secretary of the Treasury Howell Cobb (1857–1860)
  and Philip F. Thomas (1860–1861)
Secretary of War John B. Floyd (1857–1860)
Secretary of the Navy Isaac Toucey (1857–1861)
Secretary of the Interior Jacob Thompson (1857–1861)
Attorney General Jeremiah S. Black (1857–1860)
Postmaster General Aaron V. Brown (1857–1859)
  and Joseph Holt (1859–1861)

On August 16, 1858, Queen Victoria sent a telegram of greeting to President James Buchanan, successfully using the newly laid transatlantic cable for the first time. The message, "If you are the President, I am the Queen of England," took 17 hours to reach the United States. It was one of the upbeat moments of his administration. Buchanan's reply was rumored to be "HELP!"

One of the most violent events leading up to the Civil War took place during Buchanan's third year in office, and it set the tone for the remainder of his time in the White House.

On October 16, 1859, abolitionist John Brown and 21 men, including his two sons and five former slaves, set out for Harpers Ferry, Virginia (West Virginia today). After reaching the town at 4:00 am, they severed the telegraph wires and began their attack. Their goal was to occupy the federal armory and arsenal at Harpers Ferry, which they did, continuing on to capture Hall's Rifle Works, which supplied weapons to the government. The men held 60 of the town's citizens hostage in the hopes of encouraging the slaves, who were owned by those citizens, to join in Brown's plan, but none did.

The local militia surrounded Brown's gang, and one of Brown's sons was sent out to negotiate a surrender, but he was shot and killed. When news of the raid reached Buchanan's desk, he sent Marines and soldiers under Colonel Robert E. Lee to Harpers Ferry. Upon their arrival, they discovered that eight of Brown's men had been killed, and under Lee's leadership, the rebellion was stopped. In the end, Ten men were killed, including Brown's two sons and two of the former slaves, and five had escaped. Brown was wounded in the fighting. The surviving men were tried soon after in Charlestown, Virginia, and all were sentenced to death and subsequently executed. Although Brown failed at Harpers Ferry, his testimony during the trial was made public, and it helped to incite the abolitionists even more.

Buchanan's final year in office was laden with ironies. Two successful state visits by foreign dignitaries took place, which lightened the mood within the White House and gave Americans something positive to read and talk about. But outside of the bubble, the country was literally falling apart at the seams. By the time Buchanan delivered his final Annual Message to Congress on December 31, 1860, Abraham Lincoln was the President-elect, and South Carolina had seceded from the Union. Since at that time inaugurations took place four months after the presidential election, Buchanan, the lame duck, could only continue his policies with no hope of inducing Congress to any action, especially since the Republicans had gained control.

The 69-year-old Buchanan had declared that he would not be a candidate for reelection. With the sectional strife in the United States reaching a fever pitch, the Republican Party grew more powerful and gained a majority in Congress, and the Democratic Party, like the Whigs before them, split into two factions — Northern and Southern. The results of the election were as follows:

Candidates	Party	Electoral Vote
Abraham Lincoln Hannibal Hamlin	Republican	180
John C. Breckinridge Joseph Lane	Southern Democrat	72
John Bell Edward Everett	Constitutional Whig	39
Stephen A. Douglas Herschel V. Johnson	Northern Democrat	12

Contrary to what has been taught in many history classes, Buchanan's entire Cabinet did not resign when the Republicans won the election and Southern states started seceding from the Union. Only three members of his Cabinet resigned (Secretary of State Lewis Cass, Secretary of War John B. Floyd, and Secretary of the Treasury Philip F. Thomas), two were appointed to vacated positions (Attorney General Jeremiah S. Black who became Secretary of State, and Postmaster General Joseph Holt who became Secretary of War), and two remained in their posts having served from the beginning (Secretary of the Interior Jacob Thompson and Secretary of the Navy Isaac Toucey). So the make-up of his Cabinet for the last few months of his presidency was:

Secretary of State Jeremiah S. Black
Secretary of the Treasury John A. Dix
Secretary of War Joseph Holt

Secretary of the Navy Isaac Toucey
Secretary of the Interior Jacob Thompson
Attorney General Edwin M Stanton
Postmaster General Horatio King

On December 20, 1860, South Carolina seceded from the United States, which was not surprising as South Carolina had often times threatened to secede since as far back as 1833. Conventions were being assembled in other states, and from December 1860 to Lincoln's inauguration on March 4, 1861, the following states seceded from the Union: Mississippi (January 9, 1861), Florida (January 10, 1861), Alabama (January 11, 1861), Georgia (January 19, 1861), Louisiana (January 26, 1861), and Texas (February 1, 1861), giving the Confederacy seven states. By the end of May 1861, the following states joined their cause: Virginia (April 17, 1861), Arkansas (May 6, 1861), Tennessee (May 7, 1861), and North Carolina (May 21, 1861), making them eleven strong and leaving 22 states in the North. Buchanan would be the first president to preside over a divided nation, leaving a fractured union to his successor.

On January 29, 1861, Kansas was finally admitted to the Union as a free state.

After an attempt to negotiate a return to the Union was terminated by President Buchanan, South Carolina seized all public property in Charleston, and Fort Sumter was under threat of being attacked. Had it been attacked by the state, that would have been considered an act of treason committed by the government of South Carolina, and federal troops would have been ordered to counter attack. To ensure the safety of the fort, Buchanan secretly ordered the *Star of the West*, a passenger steamer with 250 troops on board dispatched immediately to the fort instead of the war steamer *USS Brooklyn*. At this early stage, all were not certain how the South Carolinians would react to a war ship arriving in the harbor to protect Fort Sumter. The passenger steamer would allow for the fort to be reinforced without suspicion. He also asked Congress for appropriations for more troops at Fort Sumter and Fort Monroe in Hampton, Virginia, reasoning that these two vulnerable military posts would not be able to defend themselves in their present conditions, but it was to no avail. Congress, fearing a military build up would only incite violence and create suspicion in the South, refused Buchanan's repeated requests for reinforcements. As a result, the North at the outset of the Civil War would be in an extremely vulnerable state with a small army and navy.

On January 8, 1861, Buchanan sent a Special Message to Congress concerning the situation in South Carolina and the federal property in the states considering secession. This final appeal to Congress for an "amicable" solution to the immediate situation in the country was the desperate attempt by the last president born in the eighteenth century and an elder statesman, who served with some of the nation's most distinguished individuals, to preserve a union that he held so dear. Unfortunately, Congress was no longer interested in what President James Buchanan had to say. Although Abraham Lincoln carried out Buchanan's policies until South Carolina attacked Fort Sumter on April 20, 1861, Buchanan was vilified for his actions and for not attacking South Carolina first.

Interestingly, throughout his entire presidency, James Buchanan implored Congress to purchase Cuba.

He also annually called for the government to look out for the well-being of the citizens of the District of Columbia as they did not have voting representation in Congress — a situation that has not changed.

But from the beginning of his term to the very end, there was one bright spot that shined from coast to coast. Whatever any American thought of President Buchanan, they truly loved the beautiful young woman who was the Lady of the White House.

Chapter 7
America's First Lady

Harriet and Lily were exhausted. They had been to every dress shop on fashionable E Street in Washington, D.C., and none of them had a gown that would suit the future White House hostess. They were seated in the last boutique on the block, being shown various designs from the store's collection, when the newly hired clerk, Rose Greenberg, returned from making the daily deposit at the bank and overheard the two young customers. She quickly ran to the back of the shop, where Loretta Saks, the proprietor, was desperately trying to come up with the right dress, but she could not get a grasp on what the customer had in mind.

The young clerk grabbed her employer's arm and excitedly asked, "Do you know who is in your store?" Loretta shook off the clerk and replied, "Some woman named Lane and her friend Lily, why?"

Rose stared at her boss in astonishment and said, "Some woman named Lane? Mrs. Saks, that is Harriet Lane and her friend Lily Macalester. Don't you read the papers?"

Loretta, who was too busy trying to find a way to keep the customers from leaving, said, "I don't have time to read the papers. I have a business to run." Rose threw her hands up, and Loretta rolled her eyes at her new employee. "Besides, they are so particular, that I am afraid I won't be able to help them, so it does not matter who they are."

Rose grabbed the dresses from Loretta's hand and told her boss, "She is the niece of President-elect James Buchanan, and the other one is the daughter of one of the richest men in the country. She is probably looking for a dress for the Inaugural Ball. If you sell her a dress, every society matron in Washington will come to your boutique."

Loretta's mouth dropped open and she asked, "That plain-looking woman is Buchanan's niece?"

"No!" replied Rose. "The other one." Rose thought for a minute and said to Loretta, "I have read a lot about her. She is very popular in Europe, and she knows fashion. Besides, if you will forgive my saying so, she is closer to my age. You let me wait on her, and if I don't sell her a dress, you can fire me."

Loretta thought for a minute and consented to the young clerk's request. Rose scanned the back room, and she spotted the dress. When the gown had arrived a few days prior, neither she, nor her boss, thought they would be able to interest anyone in purchasing it. It was too high fashion for the conservative Washington crowd. Rose grabbed the dress and exited the back room. She introduced herself to Harriet Lane and Lily Macalester.

Harriet looked at the dress, and after a frustrating day of being presented every style of gown by boutique owners who were twice her age, she knew this young clerk understood what it was she desired. She tried on the dress and looked in the mirror with pleasure. She asked Rose how long it would take to alter the dress, and the clerk said only two days. Harriet informed the proprietor that she wanted to purchase the dress, but that she wanted to make a slight change to the neckline.

Loretta assured her, "Miss Lane, I have been selling dresses in this town for almost 20 years, and what you are asking me to do to that dress will not be acceptable to the women you will be entertaining in the White House."

Harriet was taken aback, but Rose immediately rescued the situation by stepping in front of her boss and saying, "Don't you worry about a thing Miss Lane. I will personally alter the dress exactly as you wish. I think it is refreshing for someone in this town to make a bold fashion statement."

With that, Loretta excused herself to the back room. Under normal circumstances, she would have insisted on having her way, but the future lady of the White House had just purchased a $1,200 gown from her 25-year-old clerk.

For the Washington social scene, the election of James Buchanan was a godsend. Due to her belief that she and her husband were being punished for his seeking political power, Jane Appleton Pierce, "The Shadow of the White House," spent her years there as a relative recluse, while her husband drowned his sorrows. No state dinners were held, and this only exaggerated the country's dismal mood as the states became more divided over the issue of slavery.

The 26-year-old Harriet Lane, whose beauty and grace won the admiration of many in Europe, was the Bachelor President's obvious choice for official presidential hostess, and women all over the United States loved her immediately. Not since Dolly Madison, had a woman in her position been so popular. Reporting from the inauguration, the press gave Harriet Lane the title "Democratic Queen." And she was the first woman in the United States to be referred to as "First Lady." The title was first bestowed on Lane by Frank Leslie's Illustrated Newspaper in 1860, "the lady of the White House, and by courtesy, the *first lady of the land*."[32] One contemporary judged her as the perfect combination of "deference and grace." She established fashion trends, which was a first for a first lady, and the popular song "Listen to the Mockingbird" was written in her honor. In an account published in *The Washington Post* in 1892, she was recalled as "'The Golden Beauty,' as she stood beside the courtly gray old man, the President."[33]

To add to the popularity of Lane's White House, the largest and the smallest dogs to ever live there were both residents during Buchanan's administration. The President's dog was a Newfoundland named Lara, and the First Lady's companion was a tiny Nippon Terrier named Punch. Punch was a gift from the Japanese and rumored to fit in a teacup.

Lane was so popular that the United States Navy named a steam-ship revenue-cutter *The USRMCS Harriet Lane* in 1857 not long after the inauguration, and the vessel doubled as the presidential yacht. The *USRMCS Harriet Lane* was one of the first ships sent in defense of Fort Sumter in 1861. The tradition continued. In 1927, the U.S. Coast Guard commissioned the

Active Class patrol boat *Harriet Lane*, and in 1984 the *United States Coast Guard Medium Endurance Cutter (WMEC) 903 Harriet Lane* was commissioned and is still in service, based out of Portsmouth, Virginia.

It was written that "Miss Harriet Lane was an ideal White House hostess. In her regime many innovations of social usage were introduced."[34]

Miss Hetty, Buchanan's long-time housekeeper accompanied the President to Washington, but she soon tired of Lane's "imperious" style of management and returned to Lancaster to care for his Wheatland estate.

In one of her first acts as White House hostess, Lane fired most of the staff. The staff at the White House was mostly hired-out slaves when the Buchanan's arrived, and their owners were paid for their services. To avoid making slavery a direct issue of the administration, especially since Buchanan was not a slave owner, Lane dismissed all of the slave workers and hired workers who were predominantly of Irish and German descent.[35]

A strong supporter of the arts, Lane initiated "concert nights" at the White House featuring popular American artists of the time. Tents were erected on the South Lawn for such events with ice cream and cake for all who attended. During the 1850s and right up to the start of World War I, ordinary citizens could walk right up to the front door of the White House. It was not unusual for Washingtonians to have picnics on the grounds or "drop by" for a cup of coffee.

Her first state dinner, however, was not a success in the eyes of her uncle because she cancelled the liquor order and did not secure a band, but she would correct this mistake soon enough. Within months, her management and planning of events in the White House was described as "the highest degree of elegance." Lane entertained in a style that would not be witnessed again until the Kennedy administration of the 1960s. She also directed the construction of the greenhouses that were part of the White House, until Theodore Roosevelt had them torn down in 1902 to make room for the West Wing.

Lane used her position to promote three of her favorite philanthropic causes: hospital reform, prison reform and the plight of American Indians. Job Tyson, her former suitor and a member of Congress, shared her desire for prison reform and assisted her efforts through legislation and other means. With her friend, Cornelia Van Ness Roosevelt, she helped found the Roosevelt Hospital in New York. One of her other admirers was August Schell, and Lane aided him in founding the New York Institute for the Blind. In 1858, Lane helped the Chippewa Indians put a halt to the illegal liquor trade on reservations, while arranging for medical and educational facilities for American Indians. These advocacy efforts were a first for a first lady, and the Chippewa declared her "the Great Mother of the Indians."

As the country grew more divided, Lane's tasks became more difficult, but she handled them with her usual style and flare. She arranged the seating at state dinners so that Southern and Northern politicians were not at the same table. And, if she knew of those who were not on speaking terms, she seated them at different ends of the room. She was not going to have a brawl during one of her affairs! Many years after her time in the White House, Jefferson Davis said, "The White House under the administration of Buchanan approached more to my idea of a republican court in the President's house than any before, since the days of Washington."[36]

Lane also purchased many items for the White House. She was criticized for discarding some worn and damaged pieces because of their perceived historic value. In a letter dated May 20, 1858, Buchanan reminded her of the budget she had for all of her expenses:

> Learning that you were about to purchase furniture in New York, I requested Mr. Blake to furnish me a statement of the balance of the appropriation. ... The balance is $8,369.02. In making your purchases therefore, I wish you to consider that this sum must answer our purchases until the end of my term. I wish you therefore to not to expend the whole of it, but to leave enough to meet all contingencies until 4 March 1861. Any sum which may be expensed above the appropriations I shall most certainly pay out of my own pocket. I shall never ask Congress for the Deficiency.[37]

Even while keeping within her budget, she greatly impressed two royal families with her style of American hospitality.

Chapter 8
We Will Sleep in the Hallway

Harriet Lane took full advantage of two visits by foreign dignitaries that occurred in 1860 to lighten the dark mood that was settling over the United States.

In May 1860, to commemorate the first commercial treaty between the United States and Japan, members of the Japanese royal family and dignitaries paid an official state visit to the United States to exchange the treaties. Coinciding with the visit was an extended stay by the First Lady's best friend, Lily Macalester, who was also a favorite of Buchanan's.

Lily Lytle Macalester (birth unknown) was the daughter of Charles Macalester (1798-1893), a well known Philadelphia businessman and a broker in the firm of Gaw, Macalester and Company, and he was highly regarded as a guardian of selected estates. In 1834, 1835 and 1837, Macalester was appointed government director of the Second Bank of the United States in Philadelphia. He was also a friend, financier and advisor to eight U.S. Presidents from Andrew Jackson through Ulysses S. Grant. Although offered Cabinet posts, he never accepted and remained in the private sector. Macalester founded Philadelphia Presbyterian Hospital and the Macalester Presbyterian Church, and he also established Macalester College in Minnesota.

Lily married M. Berghman, a Belgian ambassador and gave birth to a daughter, Camille, who married Jose de Pedrosa, a Spanish marquis. After Berghman's death in 1874, Lily married J. Scott Laughton. She was a prominent Philadelphia hostess and was Vice Regent for the Pennsylvania Chapter of the Mount Vernon Ladies' Society from 1874 until her death in 1891.

The following excerpts are from correspondence from Lily to her father, Charles Macalester. In the letters, one can see the whirlwind of entertainment Lane provided for her guests and how truly elegant and welcoming Lane's White House was for many. Lily often referred to Harriet Lane as "Hattie," and Lane often signed her letters to Lily as "Henriquetta." On Wednesday, May 9, 1860, at 7:00 pm, Lane, Macalester and Buchanan attended a dinner at the home of British Ambassador Lord Lyons, and it was no secret that Lord Lyons was enamored with Harriet Lane:

> This has been a very gay week, the dinner at Lord Lyons' was charming the table arrangements all very elegant the company consisting of 21 persons, very select & the host, courteous gentlemanly and agreeable. He took Hattie to dinner & the Russian Minister took me ... In the evening we went to a party given by Mrs. Lewis & Miss Taylor which was delightful, where we had a nice little dance. Last evening we were at a little company at Miss Wilson's & today we have a large dinner at home.
>
> On Monday [May 14, 1860] the Japanese, it is supposed will arrive, on Wednesday the President possibly will receive them ... Today we are going under escort of the "officers in charge" to see the suite of apartments prepared for them which are said to be splendid. ... John Van Buren, was here for several days, & we saw a great deal of him, he is exceedingly agreeable & entertaining. He appears to admire Hattie greatly.
>
> The large dinner on the day I wrote, was charming. The guests were 36 in number among them Gen. Scott in full uniform, gorgeous, & dazzling to behold... After the company had dispersed the President went up to smoke a cigar in his office, & I with him, for a chat. I told him he would have to get up some sort of uniform in which to receive the Japanese, or they certainly would mistake Gen. Scott for the great man of the nation. He laughed, & said "Well I have a dressing gown that Gen. Harney gave me, perhaps that would do," but afterwards concluded, that for him to be in plain black in the midst of all the uniforms would show them that-simplicity was a mark of distinction in this Country.[38]

In the following excerpt, dated Friday, May 25, 1860, Macalester described one of the concerts hosted by Lane, "Madame De Limbourg's Matinee," in the Japanese delegation's honor. She also described the party that followed the concert with its tents on the lawn and what was served:

> Madame De Limbourg's Matinee which I wrote you was to come on Tuesday, was really charming & elegant. The garden which is very pretty, was thrown open & beautifully fixed up, a tent at one end had ices, & strawberries, & an area was lined (the brick walls) with bright chintz & filled with Lounges, chairs & etc... a table on one side with punch cakes etc. — The substantials were on a table elegantly "spread out" in the dinning room. The house is double & the dancing was in the back parlor, it was altogether, one of the most charming, & brilliant parties I have ever attended. The Japanese appeared much pleased with everything. The young prince with whom I had a small flirtation by the aid of dumb motions & my opera glass (which I showed him how to use) on Saturday recognized me most [flatteringly] & really was quite animated in his expressions of satisfaction. The others made solemn, & dignified bows to both Hattie & I. — Today the grand dinner comes off & he is to take me to table. Hattie is to be seated between two, & declares that I shall be, but I am petitioning for "A Native American," on one side of me, She vows. I shall have two Japanese & so the war is raging; how we will settle it remains to be seen.
>
> We suggested to Mr. Buchanan that it would be considered a mark of distinction by the Ambassadors, if they were placed on either side of him at the table, whereupon he threw up his hands & exclaimed, "That he would not be paid to do it," so he will be quietly ensconsed as usual between two agreeable ladies whilst Hattie & I entertain the ambassadors.
>
> When any visitor asks me about my leaving, [Mr. Buchanan] hushes them, & me right up with "She is not going for some time. I cannot possibly get along without her so that is fixed, her father has her all the time & can very well spare her to me for this little while, when I so want her."[39]

In an excerpt, dated May 26, 1860, Macalester described the official state dinner and Buchanan's admiration for her ability to entertain men who do not speak English:

[D]o you suppose after sojourning in the Executive Mansion for two months, & dashing about — all the time in the President's Carriage, I can bring myself down suddenly to the humiliation of walking the streets of Philadelphia? ...

The grand dinner to the Japanese came off yesterday & was a great success. The great Treasurer, Moruta Okatara took me to the table & the Prince Stkaharo Jugoro, sat on my left, three others were arranged along the end of the table who it also fell to my lot to entertain. So that I was talking, & motioning to five men, all through the dinner, not one of whom could speak a word of English. — The Interpreter came up every little while, & I made him convey ideas which I carried out by looks, & signs. I several times had the whole of them laughing heartily. The President complimented me extravagantly afterwards, & said "It was the most remarkable exhibition he had ever witnessed, & that he thought no other woman in the United States could have accomplished it successfully." Was that not a pretty compliment? They brought Hattie and I each a present consisting of an elegant box, containing, every variety of Japanese knick knacks, & several yards of handsome silk, which will certainly be always a very agreeable souvenir of their visit. — They are a dignified well bred people, & show marvelous tact in conforming to our usages. My friend the young Prince Stkahara Jugoro, is very bright, & interesting, asked me for my card, & to write my name on it, & then gave me his, complimented me through the Interpreter on my dancing at the Dutch Minister's, & altogether, we had quite a little flirtation.[40]

The press declared Lane's entertainment of the Japanese royalty a success, but that was just the beginning. Washington society was extremely excited in 1860 when it was learned that Queen Victoria had consented to allowing the 18-year-old Prince of Wales to extend his Canadian trip in order to tour the United States. Harriet Lane was quite pleased to be charged with preparing the social program for his stay in the nation's capital.

The prince was traveling under the name Baron Renfrew and was accompanied by a large entourage including the Duke of Newcastle. They arrived in Washington on October 3, 1860, at 4:00 pm. Thousands of spectators awaited the arrival of his train at Union Station. The receiving party consisted of Lord Lyons,

General Cass, and Lane's brothers, James and Elliot. Upon his arrival, Lord Lyons presented General Cass, who welcomed the Prince to America on behalf of the President. He was then escorted to the waiting presidential carriages and taken directly to the White House past large, cheering crowds along the way. At the White House, Buchanan, surrounded by his Cabinet and aids cordially welcomed him. For the Prince's protection, the President ordered the gates of the White House grounds to be closed and guarded by police — a rare directive.

A state dinner was given in the Prince's honor that evening at 10:00 pm, and Cabinet officers and their wives were the invited guests. During the evening, the Marine Band played American and British music for the young royal's enjoyment.[41]

During the Prince's stay, the ever-hospitable First Lady and the President gave up their bedrooms and slept in the hall, so their guests could sleep in their quarters and be as comfortable as possible.

The following morning, after Lane and the Prince went horseback riding to Georgetown Heights,[42] Buchanan escorted him to the Capitol and other sites in Washington. At noon, a public reception was held at the White House, where "the ungloved Prince was dressed in a blue coat and gray trousers and stood to the right of Buchanan." The reception almost turned into a public riot as hundreds of people clamored to be a part of the spectacle. Buchanan was dismayed to see individuals jumping in and out of the windows of the White House to get a better view of the Prince.[43] After the reception, Lane and Mrs. Jacob Thompson (wife of Secretary of the Interior Thompson) escorted the Prince to the Georgetown Visitation Convent School where she taught him how to play ten pins in the gymnasium:[44]

> His manner was somewhat bashful, and most public ceremonies apparently bored him. But when he was with Lane and the coterie of beautiful women of her set, it was noted that for the first time since he had been in the country he showed the manner of a gallant gentleman desirous of pleasing his comely host.[45]

In the gymnasium, the Prince swung himself from one end of the room to the other along the brass rings that were suspended from the ceiling, and then he climbed the ropes to everyone's amusement. He conquered the game of ten pins quickly but was "speedily out-bowled by Lane, who put his muscle to shame."[46]

When asked about Harriet Lane, the Prince of Wales said: "In person, in speech, in carriage and in manner, Harriet Lane has the charm of regal presence. She suggests to her countrymen the grand dame of European society more than any of her predecessors. Her stature is a little above the average for her sex, her figure molded in a noble cast, and her head firmly poised on neck and shoulders of queenly grace."[47]

He continued, "On public occasions the air of authority in her deportment is such that Mr. Buchanan's followers sometimes hail her as 'Our Democratic Queen.' Her beautiful hair, her violet eyes, her fine complexion, and the contour of a face and expressive mouth on which the lines of character are strongly written, mark at once a woman of both charm and power. Her voice has the bright musical intonation of a wholesome nature. Few English women can surpass her in athletic exercises, and no other 'Lady of the White House,' has been so widely copied as a model in her toilettes. Miss Lane's social direction is such that even the President's enemies regard it with admiration."[48]

That evening, Lane hosted another state dinner at 6:00 pm, with 32 guests in attendance. The Prince escorted Lane and sat to her right.[49] She arranged an after-dinner fireworks display, which she, the Prince and other guests watched from the upstairs windows.[50] The fireworks were viewed by thousands of spectators, who waited for several hours in the rain before they could commence.[51] The rain hampered the "first through fifth" places in the program, but the seventh went off without a hitch as it consisted of red, white and blue symbols of America and Great Britain. The Prince said, "Such an exhibition is deserving of the highest praise, and exceeded anything of the kind I have ever seen."[52]

On October 5, the entire party sailed to Mount Vernon on the *USRMCS Harriet Lane*, where the prince laid a wreath on the tombs of George and Martha Washington. In the evening, Lord Lyons hosted a dinner at the British embassy, where Harriet Lane was the center of attention. The following day, the Prince left for Richmond aboard the *USRMCS Harriet Lane*. He enjoyed his Washington visit so much that his mother, Queen Victoria, sent letters of gratitude to both Lane and Buchanan. The Prince sent them a portrait of himself painted by Sir John Watson Gordon, and he presented Lane with a set of autographed engravings of the royal family.[33] When Lane took the engravings with her at the end of her uncle's term in office, a furor was raised in Congress until Queen Victoria sent word that the engravings were a gift to Harriet Lane and not to the United States.

The Prince never forgot his visit to America, especially the charming First Lady.[54] Harriet Lane was invited to and attended the coronation of the former Prince of Wales as he was crowned King Edward VII of England, August 9, 1902.[55]

Apparently, the popular prince was quite the ladies' man. Queen Victoria and Prince Albert imposed a strict regimen upon Edward. Although his marriage at age twenty-two to Alexandra relieved him from some of his mother's domination, after Prince Albert's death in 1863, Victoria still would not appoint her son any official governmental role. The Prince rebelled by completely indulging himself in women, food, drink, gambling, sport and travel. His wife turned a blind eye to his extramarital activities, which had him implicated in several divorce cases.[56]

Chapter 9
Back to Wheatland

"If you are as happy, my dear sir, on entering this house as I am in leaving it and returning home, you are the happiest man in this country."

March 4, 1861, was typical of late, winter days in the nation's capital, with overcast skies and a chill in the air. The tall, stately Buchanan, robust in figure, but erect in stature and displaying the stiffly formal attire of which those around him had become accustomed — black suit, high-collar blouse and meticulously arranged, white bow tie — was standing in the south portico of the White House, overlooking the Potomac and the unfinished Washington Monument as he awaited the arrival of the President-elect. Approaching 70, he still possessed the presidential appearance that commanded attention when he entered a room. In the past four years, his hair had gone totally white, and although the features had become drawn, the jowls fuller, and the eyes more creased, he managed to present an air of distinction that few in his office had attained. It was all he had left.

Abraham Lincoln had arrived in Washington the night before by cover of darkness, disguised during most of his journey from Illinois out of fear of being assassinated by Southern sympathizers. Soldiers were posted strategically around the District with sharp-shooters standing on rooftops, including that of the White House. A carriage pulled up the drive at approximately 11:00 am. Lincoln alighted from the carriage and walked up to the entrance, removing his stove-pipe hat and extending his right hand. Buchanan saw his successor up close for the first time since he served as Secretary of State and Lincoln was serving his one term in the House of Representatives. As the two gentlemen shook hands, Buchanan could only help but notice that Lincoln stood only two inches taller than he, but his gangly appearance gave him the illusion of greater height, and next to the fullness of Buchanan, it was noticeably more evident. The younger of the two spoke first, "Good morning, Mr. President."

President James Buchanan responded, "If you are as happy, my dear sir, on entering this house as I am in leaving it and returning home, you are the happiest man in this country."[57]

In spite of the imminent danger to his life, Lincoln chose to ride in the open presidential carriage to the Capitol for his inauguration, and without fear, Buchanan, a veteran of the War of 1812, chose to accompany him.

As they proceeded east on Pennsylvania Avenue, Buchanan felt a sense of relief along with bitter disappointment that his illustrious career would be capped off by the most difficult four years of his political life. By proclaiming in his inaugural address that he would not seek a second term, he had deftly avoided a humiliating defeat. Where the Union was held together, albeit less than perfectly, four years prior, he was leaving to his successor a divided country. He did feel that he had accomplished all that he could, with a strict adherence to Constitutional doctrine, and performed the duties he was charged with executing while trying to stall a war that everyone knew was inevitable. Buchanan was incorruptible in his principles.

On that March morning, little did either man know what lay ahead would be the bloodiest four years in American history, redefining a nation and the power of the presidency. For all they knew, the new President could possibly have been the last, as the United States would no longer exist at the end of the impending conflict.

What Buchanan would not realize, as they were riding in the carriage together, was that he would be considered one of the worst presidents in U.S. history, while the man sitting next to him was destined to be regarded by many as the greatest.

For the 69-year-old Buchanan, who had enjoyed success as a Pennsylvania State Assemblyman, a member of the House of Representatives, a Senator, Minister to both Russia and England, Secretary of State, and President of the United States, March 4, 1861, was bittersweet indeed. He had achieved every goal he pursued and been held in the highest regard as an honest public servant, but during his presidency, the country had finally fallen apart. The division was inevitable. President Buchanan inherited one of the worst situations any U.S. President past or future would, and he was powerless to stop it without disregarding his Constitutionally mandated powers. As the man elected to the highest office in the land, he would shoulder the blame.

He was called a traitor by his detractors for not forcing South Carolina back into the Union. Buchanan felt that attacking one of the states presented its own host of problems. What is the state considered, an enemy, another country? And what of its inhabitants? Do they become prisoners of war? Or are they all to be prosecuted as traitors themselves?

Buchanan wanted the presidency, but gave truth to the adage, "be careful what you wish for." And, two weeks prior to Inauguration Day 1861, Jefferson Davis had been inaugurated as the President of the Confederate States of America for one six-year term.

Buchanan's ride with the President-elect was guarded by General Winfield Scott's soldiers, who had guarded Lincoln's secret trip to Washington, D.C. Lincoln took the oath of office on the East Portico, administered by Chief Justice Roger Taney for the seventh time. The Capitol itself was sheathed in scaffolding because the copper and wood "Bulfinch" dome was being replaced with a cast iron dome designed by Thomas U. Walter. The times were uncertain, and many wondered if they were witnessing the last inauguration of a United States President.

James Buchanan walked to his place while the Marine Band played "Hail to the Chief" for the last time in his honor.

As one who held the Constitution in the highest regard and loved his country as no other, it gave Buchanan great pride to see that the tradition of transferring power from one political party to another in a peaceful manner — as first demonstrated by the transition of the administration of President John Adams to that of President Thomas Jefferson in 1801 — was continuing, although seven Southern states had seceded from the Union.

Buchanan took his seat and listened to his successor deliver his inaugural address before taking the oath of office. Buchanan was pleased with the majority of the address, which reiterated his position of not interfering with the domestic affairs of any state or any individual's right to his legally owned property. Lincoln was not the outspoken abolitionist that history has claimed him to be. Contrarily, he was more concerned with preserving the Union than anything else. Lincoln continued Buchanan's policies until South Carolina attacked Fort Sumter on April 20, 1861 — policies that had labeled Buchanan a traitor in the eyes of some. Buchanan, who had aligned himself with the North after South Carolinia seceded, supported Lincoln's policies throughout the Civil War.

That afternoon, Buchanan boarded a train, and the last of the Federalist Era Presidents headed home to Wheatland, where Harriet Lane had returned a few weeks earlier.

Buchanan's retirement was uneventful as he entertained visitors and close friends and wrote his memoirs, *Mr. Buchanan's Administration, On the Eve of Rebellion*, which was published in 1866. He was the first United States President to write and publish his memoirs, and he did it without a multimillion dollar advance. In them, he defended his administration and its policies, but unfortunately, it would be years before he was vindicated. He would always be unpopular in Utah.

His last public statement was made from his deathbed on May 30, 1868, "My dear friend, I have no fear for the future. Posterity will do me justice. I have always felt, and still feel that I discharged every public duty imposed upon me conscientiously. I have no regret for any public act of my life, and history will vindicate my memory from every unjust aspersion."[58]

President James Buchanan died on June 1, 1868, in his bedroom at Wheatland after a short illness. He was 77 years old. He was buried at Woodward Hill Cemetery in Lancaster, Pennsylvania, where an American flag is still raised ever day. Buchanan would be proud. Over 4,000 citizens of Lancaster attended his funeral, where he is still Pennsylvania's favorite son.

In an article titled, "Buchanan Vindicated — The Charge that He Sympathized with Secession Denied,"[59] published in 1883 in *The Washington Post*, Buchanan biographer, George Tucker Curtis said: "It is amazing how the stale slanders of President Buchanan are repeated year to year, without the least attention to the contradiction which long since exploited them." Unfortunately, the disagreements over Buchanan's policies would continue. In 1918, his legacy, thanks to his niece's generosity, would incite another heated debate in Congress that would rival the years immediately following his time in the White House.

Buchanan left an estate that in 2005 would be worth $2,000,000. In his will, President James Buchanan bequeathed funds to Lancaster to help the widows and the poor afford fuel to heat their homes in the winter for many years after his death. And, in a codicil to his will, he left Wheatland to his favorite niece and hostess.

Chapter 10
Mrs. Harriet Lane Johnston

Once her uncle had retired, Harriet Lane was no longer occupied with the glamorous life of a political hostess. Now in her mid-thirties, Lane's life had quieted enough for her to concentrate on herself.

Although the popular and beautiful Harriet Lane had been courted for many years by several eligible suitors, it was the 35-year-old, Baltimore banker, Henry Elliot Johnston, who won her heart. She met Johnston years earlier while vacationing in Bedford Springs, Pennsylvania. The fact that her uncle heartily approved of the young man did not hurt his chances.

On January 11, 1866, in the parlor at Wheatland and at the age of 36, America's First Lady became Mrs. Harriet Lane Johnston. It was one of the happiest moments of President James Buchanan's retirement. The following announcement appeared in *The New York Times* on January 22, 1866:

> The marriage of Miss Harriet Lane, niece of Ex-President Buchanan, to Henry E. Johnston, Esq., transpired at Wheatland, Mr. Buchanan's residence, near Lancaster at 1 o'clock P. M. on Thursday last. The ceremony was performed by Rev. E.Y. Buchanan (brother of the Ex-President), pastor of Trinity Church, near the city, and the fair bride was given away by her venerable uncle. Among the invited guests were the following: Rev. E.Y. Johnston and Lady, and four daughters; Mr. J. Buchanan Henry, private secretary of the president for two years from 1857; Mr. and Mrs. Thos. E. Franklin; Dr. H. Carpenter; Mrs. J.B. Lane, Rev. B. Keenan, of the Catholic Church; Rev. Mr. Powell of the

Presbyterian Church, all of Lancaster; Mr. and Mrs. Brinton;
Dr. and Mrs. Nevin, and the Misses of Nevin; Capt. Nevin,
late of the United States Army; Mr. and Misses Johnston of
Baltimore, brother and sisters of the groom; and Charles
Macalester, of [Philadelphia], and Augustus Schell of New
York.

After the ceremony, the company sat down to dinner
prepared by AUGUSTIN in his best manner, and in the
evening the newly married twain started for Philadelphia,
where they remained until Friday, when they left for
Baltimore. The Ex-President was in fine health, and as happy
as could be expected at a separation from a lady to whom
he was so much attached, and whose refinement and
accomplishments, and rare discrimination have been such
invaluable agencies to him in his public, especially in his
presidential career, and have been faithful
accompaniments of his declining years. Mr. Johnston, now
the husband of the former lady of the White House, is a
gentleman of large fortune in Baltimore, and a banker by
avocation.[60]

The Johnstons honeymooned in Cuba and made their home
on Park Avenue in Baltimore. Henry Elliot Johnston was a
partner in the banking house of Johnston Brothers & Co., located
at 198 Baltimore Street.

Upon hearing of her marriage, Catherine Ellis wrote the
following to Lane on April 13, 1866. Her reference to the prior
four years speaks of the Civil War. During the War, General
John A. Dix, who was a friend of Buchanan's and a Lane
admirer, would use diplomatic channels to have Lane's letters
delivered to Ellis. The letters went to Alabama via Richmond,
while Dix was stationed at Fort Monroe, Virginia:

By a happy chance the cards with your new name found
me at last, and although I had heard of your marriage, the
reality of the event impresses me deeply. I have and do
wish you every blessing for this life and greater blessings
hereafter. My congratulations shall not be mired with any
mention of the past four years. I expect to spend the
summer in Camden, and propose an opportunity to meet
you again. How much I shall have to ask, how much to tell.
Present me to your husband and believe me that I love you
as I ever did.[61]

She received the following letter, on June 10, 1866, from her dear friend, Lily, whose father attended the wedding:

> I would long since have written a reply to your kind letter, and to offer you my most affectionate and heartfelt wishes for your happiness had I not been presented first by Mr. Bergman's illness, and subsequently by my own indisposition. As a married wife which I wrote father last week, I begged him to explain this to you.
>
> How much I regret being away at this time dear Hattie. I have so many loving things to say to you which seem so [illegible] when committed to paper. When I received your letter mentioning that you really were to be married my thoughts went back to our past acquaintance then to our growing friendship and intimacy. To all the many many happy hours we have passed together to the kindness that has always existed between us and which has never been clouded by a doubt on either side and from my own heart dearest Hattie with a prayer that this might always continue and that the friendship that has existed so long much to unchangingly might never while we have been betrothen.
>
> I need not hope that you have chosen a happy destiny. I know you have the [advantage] of so many years as [a happy person] that such is the case and my appreciation of Mr. Johnston's many agreeable qualities more than support the belief I only wish I have been able [to attend].
> ...
> I learned that you really had decided to be married this winter, but I hope soon ... some obliging might — who will take charge of a party when you have a moment to write me.
>
> Believe me always most truly and affectionately, your sincere friend.[62]

Lane's life seemed picture perfect when she gave birth to her first child, James Buchanan Johnston, in November 1866, ten months after her wedding. But the next 18 years would bring back the recurring theme of death that ran through her entire life, starting with the death of her beloved uncle and guardian, President James Buchanan, in June 1868. She inherited Wheatland, which she and her husband maintained as a summer home for the next 16 years. Little more than a year later, in 1870, she gave birth to her second son, Henry Elliot Johnston, Jr.

Hindering her enjoyment of life as wife and mother was a dispute with James Buchanan biographer, William B. Reed, that lasted ten years. Reed, whom Buchanan had designated his biographer through a codicil in his will, and her uncle Reverend Edward Buchanan, were in constant conflict with Lane over the private correspondence and papers of the late President. Reed would never complete the work, and the papers would never be completely recovered. What was not recovered of them ended up in a warehouse in New York where they were destroyed in a fire in the early part of the twentieth century. Some theories have Reed finding a note among the papers demanding they be destroyed upon the death of Buchanan and his doing just that. Another version has Buchanan destroying much of his own personal correspondence after completing his memoirs. Either version explains the scant remaining personal correspondence of President James Buchanan.

Tragedy struck again on March 25, 1881, when her son, James Buchanan Johnston, died of rheumatic fever at the age of 14. The Johnstons had a stained glass window depicting the archangel Michael, created and donated to the Lancaster Episcopal Church. Many said the angel in the window looked exactly like James. When they learned that their other son, Henry, was also suffering from rheumatic fever, they traveled to Paris, hoping the warm weather would help his condition. It did not. On October 30, 1882, Lane's 12-year-old son, Henry Elliot Johnston, Jr., died while they were in Paris.

Such tragedy would have destroyed a weaker soul, but the strong willed and generous Harriet Lane Johnston channeled her sorrow in a positive direction. While traveling with their son's remains back to the United States, the Johnstons discussed how they could best remember their children's lives. At the time, there were no hospitals or doctors who specialized in the treatment of children and childhood illnesses. As a result, they founded the Harriet Lane Home for Invalid Children in Baltimore, whose sole purpose was the care of children with chronic diseases. The Harriet Lane Home for Invalid Children officially became the Pediatric Training Center for Johns Hopkins University in 1912, thus making it the first American pediatrics institution. It is now the Teaching and Research Pediatrics Center of the Johns Hopkins School of Medicine. The *Harriet Lane Handbook: A Manual for Pediatric Officers* is still published annually, and The Harriet Lane Outpatient Clinics serve thousands of children worldwide to this day.

On May 5, 1884, three years after the death of her first-born son, Mrs. Harriet Lane Johnston became a widow as her husband, Henry Elliot Johnston, died unexpectedly from pneumonia. The 54-year-old former Lady of the White House was alone for the first time in her life.

The following appeared in *The Washington Post* on November 23, 1884:

> The first bachelor President had quite a brilliant administration socially. His niece, Harriet Lane, was in many respects a magnificent woman. Her appearance was striking and her manner winning. Intellectually, she was very strong, and she presided over her uncle's household with a dignity and grace that has landed her name down to posterity as one of the best female characters ever in the White House. She has seen great sorrow since those days. Her uncle, whom she loved as a father, has passed away, and her two little boys, the fruit of her happy marriage, have both died within the past three years. Her husband also departed this life suddenly within the past year, and the brilliant mistress of the White House of a little more than a quarter of a century ago is a childless widow.[63]

One bright spot during this dark three-year period was the publication of George T. Curtis's biography of President James Buchanan in 1883, which she felt had vindicated her uncle as a patriot and statesman.

Johnston sold both Wheatland and her home on Park Avenue in Baltimore, along with most of her possessions, donating many of her valuable European works of art to the Smithsonian Institute, and as a result, she was called the "First Lady of the National Collection of Fine Arts." Although the majority of her paintings were considered minor works, her gift set a precedent for other collectors in the United States to donate their artwork to museums throughout the country.

To make a new start, she moved to a townhouse next to Farragut Square, located at 1730 K Street NW, Washington, D.C., and for the remainder of her life, her name would be misspelled in the Washington City Directory as "Johnson, Harriet Lane."

Once a residential district, the site of her first home in Washington was on the southwest corner of the intersection of Connecticut Avenue and K Street. It is now the home of a newly constructed office building, the second to be built at that address. Her home faced north, and from her east side windows, she could see Farragut Square. From her front windows facing north, she had a view of the enormous home of Alexander Robey Shepherd, otherwise known as "Boss Shepherd." His home was on the northeast corner of the same intersection and is now the home of a retail drug store and an office building as well. The neighborhood was known at the time as "Shepherd's Row." Shepherd had transformed the city by literally tearing up the infrastructure and installing sewers and other improvements while Governor of Washington. Unfortunately, Shepherd's financial practices were the reason Congress stripped the District of its home rule in 1896, which was partially restored in the mid-1960s.

In the fall of 1894, Lane moved to a larger home on the northeast corner of the intersection of 18th Street and I Street NW, at 1737 I Street. The second home was catty-corner to the first home on the same block but faced south, and an office building is also located on this site today. Upon moving into her new I Street address, the following announcement appeared:

> Mrs. Harriet Lane Johnston, accompanied by her [cousin] Miss Kennedy, has left the city and is now settled for the summer in Charlestown, W. VA. When Mrs. Johnston returns to the city in the autumn she will take possession of her new home, the Aullick Palmer house, which she purchased some months since, and which for some time past has been in the hands of workmen, who have almost completely revolutionized the interior. The exterior of the house has undergone many alterations as well. The most notable in this respect is the removal of the large portico that formerly ornamented the south [facing I Street NW] and west [facing 18th Street NW] fronts of the house. On the west side a number of additional windows have been cut, while on the east side three or four windows have been bricked up. The entrance will be modernized and reached by a short flight of stone steps. When a coat of paint is added to the various

other changes on the exterior, the house will bear but slight resemblance to its former self.[64]

Both of Lane's Washington, D.C., residences were less than four blocks from her former residence, the White House. After 23 years, America's First Lady would return to make her mark on Washington society once again, as the first Democrat since Buchanan was now President of the United States.

It was not like Lane to wallow in self-pity. Her life was practically guided by death, beginning with the death of Anne Caroline Coleman, through the deaths of her parents, her uncle and guardian, her own young sons and the man who finally won her heart. With each tragedy, she lifted herself up, and with her generosity, grace, and optimism, she emerged from the depths of sorrow to live the life she was so fortunate to have and share that life with others. With her head held high and her signature style, she was and would always be America's First Lady.

Rose Greenberg returned from her errand at the bank and walked into the boutique on E Street, where she had worked for more than 19 years. She noticed there were two women in the store, and she walked into the back room looking for Mary Summers, the young clerk who had only worked there a few weeks. Mary was obviously a little frazzled, and Rose asked her what was wrong.

"It is those two women. One of them wants a dress for a state dinner at the White House, but I cannot seem to help her," Mary told her. Rose assured Mary that everything would be fine and offered to take over, and the young clerk was all too happy to relieve herself of the two patrons.

Rose reemerged from the back room as the two women were looking out the window. One of the women said to the other, "Lily, this street has really changed. There used to be a stable right over there." Rose thought for a minute that it could not be, but she had read in the paper that the former First Lady had moved back to Washington, D.C.

Rose cleared her throat, and the women turned around. Rose recognized them immediately. Both of them had turned gray, but little else had changed.

Harriet Lane Johnston looked at her and asked, "Rose, do you still work here?"

Rose told her that she had bought the shop in 1876, which meant she had owned it for ten years. The ladies conversed for some time, catching up on the happenings in all of their lives. Lily Macalester was now Lily Laughton with a married daughter and a grandchild.

The loyal customer told Rose, "Your young clerk could not quite grasp what I want. It seems that everywhere I go, I am shown mourning dresses for the mature woman. You always knew what I liked. Do you have something that would suit my taste?"

Rose assured her she did. She excused herself to the back where Mary had been listening behind the curtain. She watched as Rose picked through their stock of formal gowns and chose the most elegant dress in the collection — a $1,400 gown imported directly from Paris.

Rose strode out of the back room and displayed the exquisite, black velvet, off-the-shoulder gown, with a bodice adorned with tiny crystal beads. The former White House hostess tried on the dress and looked at herself in the mirror. Lily told her she looked absolutely regal.

Harriet Lane Johnston, who was quite pleased herself, said to Rose, "I love it ... however, I want to make one small change to the neckline."

Chapter 11
The Ladies Who Lunch

Francis Folsom Cleveland, the 22-year-old bride of President Grover Cleveland, was walking arm and arm with her husband to the East Room for her first official state dinner since she married the 49-year-old President a few months prior on June 2, 1886. The naturally confident First Lady was unusually jumpy this evening, wondering if she had chosen the right menu, wine and music for the evening. "Why did I choose the East Room and not the State Dining Room?" she thought. The President took notice of her uneasiness and patted her hand lovingly as they made their way down the hall. He smiled at her, and she forced a smile back, while going over all the details in her head. Normally, she would be relaxed at this point, knowing that she had done everything possible to ensure the evening would proceed without a hitch. After all, she had hosted a few state dinners while engaged to the President, and even planned their Blue Room wedding — a first for the White House. But on this particular evening, she needed for everything to be perfect.

Upon seeing the First Couple approach his position at the entrance to the East Room, the chief usher scanned the room to be sure his well trained staff were at their posts. He knew the building better than the back of his hand as he had been at his post for more than 30 years. He had given all the staff detailed instructions earlier that evening, as he inspected every button, checked every shoe, and straightened every bow tie. He even had the doorman practice his bow several times before he was satisfied. When he was asked how they would know when the guest of honor arrived, he told them to watch for the most regal figure they had ever seen. With the First Couple standing next to him, he announced, "Ladies and Gentleman, the President of the United States and the First Lady," and the invited guests applauded while the Marine Band struck up "Hail to the Chief."

As the Clevelands made their way around the room and greeted their guests, a carriage pulled up the drive. The melody that could be heard outside was all too familiar to the handsome, white haired woman, alighting from her carriage at the South Portico. It was not like her to be late, but she too was a bit nervous. She had to solicit the aid of her cousin, May Kennedy, in buttoning her off-the-shoulder, black velvet dress and fastening the clasps on both her diamond necklace and brooch. As she walked through the entrance, word of her arrival quickly made its way through the mansion, and each of the staff managed to make his or her way to the hallway to catch a glimpse of the latest guest. The doorman took her wrap and bowed perfectly. She thanked him and slowly made her way to the East Room, absorbing the ambiance and admiring how the current First Lady had been able to redecorate the White House in such a short period. But she was not surprised at the young bride's energy, for over a quarter century earlier, another vivacious young woman had exhibited the same enthusiasm when discharging her own duties as White House hostess.

The chief usher recognized her immediately. Her perfectly coiffed hair, held in place with diamond-adorned combs, may have turned white, but her beautiful face and magnificent figure had defied the years. He paused for a moment to take in the sight that stood next to him, and in a gesture saved for a few, he leaned down, winked, and then whispered in her ear, "It is so good to have you back." The lady looked up at him and smiled, "Thank you, Robert. It is good to be back."

As the guests took notice of the striking woman standing next to the chief usher, the room grew quiet. For the first time in over a quarter century, Robert announced slowly and deliberately, "Ladies and Gentleman, Mrs. Harriet Lane Johnston," and the Marine Band struck up "Listen to the Mockingbird."

The beautiful young woman, whose ample bosom had almost caused a scandal on a March evening long ago, floated into the room, and at that moment, the former "Democratic Queen" established herself as the "Grand Dame of Washington Society."

She greeted each guest as if she had never left, and the *beau monde* welcomed her back with open arms. That evening at the White House, in the fall of 1886, marked a triumphant return for America's First Lady.

So gracious was the former White House hostess that by the end of the evening, she put her young successor at great ease as she not only complimented the décor, the food, the wine and the band, but she also declared the First Lady's choice of the East Room an absolute stroke of genius. As a result, Mrs. Cleveland would be sure to invite her predecessor back at every opportunity.

The following day and for the rest of her life, absolutely no Washington guest list was complete without the name Mrs. Harriet Lane Johnston. Open the society pages of *The Washington Post* from 1886 to the very beginning of the twentieth century and scarcely a week would go by without the mention of the former First Lady. She was invited to, and hosted, Washington's most fashionable events for 16 years. In addition, the ever-generous Lane was a patroness of charities for children and other worthy causes dear to her heart.

On December 9, 1894, in an article titled "Our Wealthy Widows — Prominent Washington Society," the following was written about the 64-year-old Harriet Lane Johnston:

> A conspicuous figure in Washington society, a woman representing a great generation with the grace, dignity and bearing of a thorough woman of the world, whose ideas are always kept quite up to date is Mrs. Harriet Lane Johnston. There is no more elegant figure in the official and social gatherings during the season than the niece of President James Buchanan.[65]

From the Society Pages — Selected Happenings in Washington, D. C. (1888-1902)

On April 22, 1888, Lily Lytle Macalester Berghman Laughton and "Mr. and Mrs. Pelroso returned early in the week from a fortnight stay at Atlantic City." Mrs. Laughton was greatly improved in health and was now giving much of her time in preparing for the annual council of the vice-regents of the Mount Vernon Ladies' Society, which held its sessions the following month. Mrs. Harriet Lane Johnston was then her guest, and the day before Mrs. Laughton and Mrs. Johnston had a few friends meet them for lunch.[66]

HL

President Grover Cleveland and his young wife, Francis Folsome Cleveland, on January 12, 1894, received the diplomatic corps. Among the guests was Mrs. Harriet Lane Johnston, who was wearing a gown of black velvet, point lace and diamonds.[67]

HL

Mrs. Francis Cleveland accepted the invitation of Mrs. Harriet Lane Johnston to attend the performance of "Mustapha," to be given at Albaugh's Monday night, February 23, 1894, by the "Paint and Powder" Club of Baltimore. On that occasion, the First Lady occupied a seat in Mrs. Harriet Lane Johnston's box.[68]

HL

A reception for the "Alaskan Esquimuax" (Eskimos) was held in the Blue Room of the White House, March 3, 1894, and was hosted by Mrs. Francis Cleveland. After the Esquimaux departed, the First Lady held a reception in the Red Room, where she served a luncheon of tea, coffee, wafers, sandwiches and cake to her guests including Mrs. Harriet Lane Johnston.[69]

HL

The Hunt Club Ball, one of the most brilliant and picturesque events of the social season was held in Chevy Chase on December 28, 1894. Hundreds of guests, including Mrs. Harriet Lane Johnston, dressed in the most elegant gowns and enjoyed fine dining in the beautiful and lavishly decorated ballroom.[70]

ℋℒ

On February 5, 1897, preparations had already commenced for the Washington Assembly Ball, which was to take place at the Arlington on the evening of February 8. No one, who was present at the last ball, failed to recall the exquisite decorations of the prior year's ball. The governors planned an event that eclipsed the previous efforts. Mrs. Harriet Lane Johnston received the guests and Lt. Buckingham of the Navy led the cotillion.[71]

ℋℒ

The British Ambassador and Lady Pauncefote hosted a dinner at the British Embassy on May 24, 1897, to commemorate the birthday of Queen Victoria. The tables were "superb with handsome appointments," and graced with a "magnificent silver service" and silver candelabras. Among the invited guests was one of the Queen's favorite Americans, Mrs. Harriet Lane Johnston.[72]

ℋℒ

Mrs. Leiter hosted a cotillion, January 14, 1898, in honor of her youngest daughter, Miss Daisy, who led the dances with Mr. Craig Wadsworth of New York. There were 300 guests in attendance, including Mrs. Harriet Lane Johnston.[73]

ℋℒ

The members of the Alibi Club hosted their Annual Thanksgiving Day Tea on November 30, 1899. They gathered in the "quaint old clubhouse, which had been the scene of many illustrious entertainments." As a supper club with a limited membership, the Alibi Club, which included the "choicest spirits" of the capital, enjoyed an international reputation and was one of the "smartest and happiest institutions in Washington life." For years, the Alibi Tea opened the social season and although antedated by several debutante affairs in 1899, the invited guests were "by far the most distinguished" ever to attend the annual tea. Obviously, Mrs. Harriet Lane Johnston was present to kick off the social season.[74]

HL

On March 2, 1900, Mr. and Mrs. Potter Palmer were honored at a luncheon hosted by the Minister of Austria and Baroness Hengelmuller. Among their guests were Lady Poncefote, the Belgian Minister and Countess Lichtervelde, Mr. and Mrs. Richardson, Mrs. Patrick D. Grant, Count Taranosky, Baron Ambrozy, and of course, Mrs. Harriet Lane Johnston.[75]

HL

Representative and Mrs. Olmsted of Pennsylvania hosted a "delightful reception" at the Chevy Chase Club on May 10, 1900, adding "another pretty outdoor fete to the list of delightful affairs" for which the 1900 social season was known. Mrs. Harriet Lane Johnston was among the invited guests.[76]

HL

The Annual Charity Ball for the Children of the Poor was held on January 28, 1901. "No charity appeals more strongly to the best in nature than that which provides for the maimed and helpless little children of the poor." At the charity ball, which was held at the Arlington, for the Children's Hospital, "two fine bands furnished the music, so that the non-dancing set" could be entertained with the special program. "The supper was particularly fine." The patronesses included Mrs. Hay, Mrs. Root, Mrs. Gage, Lady Poncefote, Duchess de Arcos, and Mrs. Harriet Lane Johnston.[77]

HL

"One of the foremost of the Lenten entertainments in which fashion and charity love to unite," was the play and concert by a company of "distinguished amateurs on Friday, March

8, 1901." The entertainment benefited the Woman's Exchange, which was sadly in need of funds and was a "most deserving charity." The patronesses of the affair included Lady Poncefote, Mrs. John Hay, Baroness Hengelmuller, and Mrs. Harriet Lane Johnston.[78]

HL

Mrs. Roosevelt, First Lady of the White House, hosted a tea on December 23, 1901, from 4:00–6:00 pm, in honor of Miss Carew and her guests. "The company were welcomed in the Blue Parlor, which was more elaborately decorated than on any former occasion of the present administration." Mrs. Harriet Lane Johnston and her niece, Miss Kennedy, were among the invited guests and enjoyed the afternoon immensely.[79]

HL

Miss Wilson, daughter of the Secretary of Agriculture, hosted a luncheon in honor of Miss Fanny Reed of Paris, who was the guest of Mrs. Thomas Walsh, on January 18, 1902. Mrs. Harriet Lane Johnston was there to welcome Miss Reed.[80]

HL

On May 15, 1902, the Society of Washington Artists and the Washington Architectural Club held their opening reception of the Spring exhibition at the Corcoran Gallery of Art. The annual private viewing was always a highlight of the social season. Admission was entirely by card with the guests presenting their invitations at the New York Avenue entrance. One of the evening's hostesses was Mrs. Harriet Lane Johnston,[81] making her final public appearance in Washington society.

HL

In the summer of 1902, Mrs. Harriet Lane Johnston, traveled to England as an invited guest to attend the coronation of the former Prince of Wales, which was held on August 9. Her life had come full circle, for she sailed across the Atlantic to witness the coronation of the Prince as King Edward VII of England. He had visited her when she was the "The Democratic Queen." It was a fitting final mention of America's First Lady in the society pages.

Chapter 12
America Says Goodbye to Her First Lady

Late in the afternoon, the elderly woman held her head up high as she made her way to the front porch. She was nearing the end of her days, yet the few friends and relatives, who were keeping her company these last few weeks, never saw her look more beautiful. Her cousin offered assistance, but the proud lady shook her head as she slowly walked outside. She seated herself on her favorite Adirondack chair while her cousin stood beside her. She watched the setting sun and thought back to the extraordinary life she led, the people she met, the places she visited, and the loved ones who had gone before her. Neither woman spoke as words were not necessary.

The sun disappeared into the horizon, and America's First Lady closed her eyes.

In the fall of 1902, Harriet Lane Johnston was diagnosed with cancer. For the next few months, she would get her affairs in order, adding several codicils to her will, looking out for the well-being of her remaining relatives. Also among her concerns was the viability of the Harriet Lane Home for Invalid Children and other worthwhile causes that were dear to her heart. Typical of the way she had conducted her life, Lane was determined to find something positive to do in the face of a tragedy.

In the spring of 1903, she traveled one last time to her summer home in Narragansett, Rhode Island, as she wished to be comfortable during her final days. On Friday, July 3, 1903, America's First Lady died after a long and courageous battle. She was 73 years old.

Her funeral took place on Monday, July 6, 1903. Harriet Lane Johnston was buried at Green Mount Cemetery in Baltimore alongside her husband and her two sons.

The following are excerpts of obituaries that appeared the day after Harriet Lane died, Saturday, July 4, 1903, the 127th birthday of the United States:

Death of Buchanan's Niece —
Mrs. Harriet Lane Johnston Dies After Long Illness

Pittsburgh, PA, July 3 — Word was received here tonight by relatives of the family that Mrs. Harriet Lane Johnston, niece of President James Buchanan, died at Narragansett Pier late this evening. Her remains will be taken to Baltimore and buried beside her husband and children on Monday, July 6.

As Harriet Lane, Mrs. Johnston, was the great beauty during the administration of her uncle, President Buchanan and she has taken rank as easily one of the most interesting of the "four year queens" who have ruled the Presidential Mansion.

Despite the obstacles of a political nature, the beautiful Harriet Lane made the White House a center of social activity and by her tact did much to hold beneath the surface the hostile sentiment rising in official circles.

The most notable of Harriet Lane's White House career was her entertainment of the Prince of Wales, now King Edward VII, upon the occasion of his visit to this country.

The marriage of Harriet Lane to Mr. Johnston, a member of an old Baltimore family, took place at Wheatland, the Buchanan estate in Lancaster, Pa., and was of course one of the most famous social events of the period.

After a few years of happiness, however, Mrs. Johnston sustained a [triple] bereavement in the loss of her husband

and two sons. For a long time past, she resided in Washington. Mrs. Johnston had as her companion her cousin, Miss Kennedy, and their home is filled with interesting art objects and souvenirs among the number being the large engravings of the royal family, which were sent by the Prince of Wales as a present to Miss Lane after his return from his American tour.

When upon her departure from the White House, Miss Lane took these pictures to her own home a storm of protest was raised by persons who believed that the pictures had been presented to the American nation, but the British government hastened to give assurances that the engravings had been intended as a personal gift to Miss Lane.[82]

Harriet Lane Johnston Dies at Narragansett — Mistress of the White House in Administration of Her Uncle President James Buchanan

... Harriet Lane was a famous name in Washington just before the Civil War, and she is one of the best remembered mistresses of the White House. She was born in Mercersburg, Penn. ... [S]he was brought up by her uncle with affectionate care.

Mr. Buchanan's letters to his niece, when she was a school girl and after Miss Lane had grown up, written almost daily during her absences from him give a charming picture of the Buchanan's family life. ...

When Mr. Buchanan became President, Miss Lane presided over the White House with grace and dignity."[83]

Harriet Lane Johnston, whose life seemed guided by tragedy, used her own death to promote her worthy causes and perpetuate the memory of her loving family. And in the end, she was determined to have the last word on the legacy of her beloved uncle.

Chapter 13
The Legacy of
America's First Lady

There are several documents that have been influential in the history of the United States, and the 34-page Last Will and Testament of Harriet Lane Johnston is one of them. She left an estate, which in 2005 would be worth close to $11,500,000. Her bequests had an incredible impact on the cities of Baltimore and Washington, D.C., as Lane's generosity sustained a hospital for terminally ill children, established a school for boys, saved a national gallery, and built a monument to a United States President. And more than 100 years after the first reading of her will, almost all of what she established as part of her legacy survives to this day.

In memory of her dear friend Lily Macalester and her visit with the Prince, Lane bequeathed to the "Regent and Ladies of the Mount Vernon Association, to be placed and kept in the Mansion House of General Washington at Mount Vernon, the painting by Rossiter of the visit of President Buchanan and the Prince of Wales to Mount Vernon."[84]

To be sure her uncle was portrayed in his best likeness, she left to the United States of America "to be placed and kept in the Executive Mansion, the bust of President Buchanan and the portrait of him painted before his going to Russia as Minister of the United States to that country." The portrait was considered to be the best likeness of him ever painted, and she ventured to express the wish that this portrait may be substituted for any portrait that was in the Executive Mansion at the time of her death.[85] It is still the official portrait of Buchanan and can be viewed on the White House website.

The Harriet Lane Home for Invalid Children was the largest beneficiary of her will, as she left to them the portrait in oil of her husband Henry E. Johnston in his youth, the portraits of her sons and other articles connected with them to be placed in a room in the Home set apart for the reception and custody of the articles. She also left them all of her bed and table linens, pictures, books and furniture that "were suitable for its uses and purposes" that were not left to any of her relatives. Most importantly, any money not earmarked for anyone else or any other charity was to go to the Harriet Lane Home. If any of her beneficiaries were to die or refuse her bequests, the funds were to revert back to the Home, including a certain controversial bequest worth $100,000.[86] As if that were not enough, the balance of her husband's remaining estate was also left for the Harriet Lane Home: "The increase of my separate estate having been entirely due to the care and attention of my late husband it is my wish that it should go to the Harriet Lane Home for Invalid Children of the City of Baltimore."[87]

In 1912, when the Harriet Lane Residency Program at Johns Hopkins University officially opened, it consisted of only two interns, and the number of daily patient visits approximated 30. As of 2005, the resident classes increased to 24-25 members, and the number of daily patient visits averaged 70-80. More than 1,200 pediatricians have been trained in the Harriet Lane Residency Program since its inception. "The Harriet Lane Residency program has influenced pediatric care and training of residents through the publication of the *Harriet Lane Handbook*." The handbook is still in print and updated on a regular basis. Harrison Spencer, M.D., Harriet Lane House Staff (1951), proposed the idea for a handbook written by the Harriet Lane Home staff for their successors. By tradition, the pediatric chief residents have been the editors of subsequent editions. The mission of this project was to document how to perform a test, to supply reference data, and to compile a list of drugs and pediatric dosages. Today, the demand for this manual is extraordinary with over 50,000 copies sold each year.[88]

To Johns Hopkins University, she bequeathed $60,000 to found and perpetually maintain three free scholarships to be called respectively the "Henry E. Johnston," the "James Buchanan Johnston," and the "Henry E. Johnston, Jr.," scholarships "to be awarded to poor youths under such conditions as the University established."[89] The scholarships were awarded through the late 1930s. To the Church Home Infirmary of the City of Baltimore, Lane left $2,000 to erect and furnish a ward for boys, as a memorial to her husband, which was to be known and designated as the "Henry E. Johnston Ward for Boys."

In the second largest bequest of her will, and in memory of her two sons, she left $300,000 for the establishment of a "school for choir boys." The money was left to the Protestant Episcopal Cathedral Foundation, which was chartered by an act of Congress on January 6, 1893. The National Cathedral, as it was to become, was also the site of the first building at St. Albans School. On June 1, 1905, the cornerstone of the Lane-Johnston Building was laid by Bishop William Paret.[90] The firm of York & Sawyer of New York was chosen to design the school, which was located near Massachusetts Avenue on the east side of the Cathedral, and the building was made of Potomac Stone.

"Two hundred choir boys, nearly all the city clergy in their vestments, twelve men from the Marine Band and Bishop Satterlee, in full canonicals, made up the procession, which started from the little Church of St. Albans at 3:30 pm," on May 9, 1907, which was the anniversary of Harriet Lane's birth, to dedicate the almost completed building.[91] During the ceremony, the Bishop said, "Since the days of President Buchanan, when Mrs. Johnston graced the White House, she has been a prominent figure in the City of Washington, always an influence, attractive and magnetic, an influence for unbounded good … grant that her ideal of holy music, consecrated to the service of Almighty God may not fade away."[92] In 1909, the school opened its doors. The original Lane-Johnston Building is still the main building of the school, and the St. Albans School for Washington Cathedral Choir Boys is one of the premiere educational institutions in Washington, D.C.

Although most of her bequests were welcomed with open arms, one was refused within days of her death. Harriet Lane left the bulk of her artwork to the Corcoran Gallery of Art, which was extremely generous, considering there were 29 paintings along with other items of interest including:

> The portrait of King Edward VII, by Sir John Watson Gordon, painted for President Buchanan and sent to him after Prince of Wales' visit
>
> The framed letter of presentation from the Prince
>
> The portrait of James Buchanan Johnston painted when about fourteen years of age by Harper Pennington
>
> The marble bust of President Buchanan by Dexter of Boston
>
> The first message sent over the Atlantic Cable from Queen Victoria and answered by President Buchanan, framed
>
> The photograph, framed, of Queen Victoria, presented to Harriet Lane Johnston by her Majesty in June, 1898[93]

Unfortunately, the problems started with the conditions for acceptance of her collection. Lane's will stated that the articles should be kept together in a room, provided for the purpose, in the Corcoran Gallery of Art, and to be designated as "The Harriet Lane Johnston Collection." Not only that, but the place of deposit was to be selected and approved by Mr. Ralph C. Johnson and Mr. Blakeslee of New York. She further provided that "in the event that the Government of the United States shall establish in the City of Washington a National Art Gallery, that the said articles shall, upon the establishment of said National Art Gallery, be, by the said Trustees of the Corcoran Gallery of Art and their successors, delivered to the said National Art Gallery, and upon such delivery shall become the absolute property of the said National Art Gallery established by the United States."[94]

What followed was added to her will a few days before she died:

> The Corcoran Gallery of Art shall build an annex to the Art Gallery, to be approved by the said Mr. Blakeslee ... which said annex shall not be provided with any means for artificial heat and shall be so constructed and arranged as to protect, as far as possible from the heat of Summer the articles therein deposited. My reason for this condition is

that many of the said pictures bequeathed to the said
Trustees of the Corcoran Gallery of Art are of a character to
become cracked and ultimately ruined if deposited in a
place subject to the heat ordinarily maintained in said Art
Gallery, and are such as require, for their preservation, to be
kept in a depository of low temperature; and it is my belief
that, if a suitable annex, as above described be provided,
the said Trustees will be the recipients of other gifts of
valuable paintings which the owners would be unwilling to
have deposited in the present Gallery subject to the thermal
conditions there existing.[95]

The conditions were too much for the Corcoran Gallery to
accept, and an article relayed the news to the public on July 12,
1903. A reporter from *The Washington Post* wrote, "There is not
the slightest possibility that the Harriet Lane Johnston bequest of
29 pictures will be accepted by the Corcoran Gallery of Art."[96]
The principal reason was that the Corcoran figured the
stipulations would cost more than the collection's worth. But
that was not the end of it for Lane's collection, for she stipulated
that it be donated to a "National Art Gallery" when one was
established. When the Corcoran refused the collection, the
trustees of Lane's estate refused to release the collection, and a
legal battle ensued.

A national gallery still did not exist in Washington, D.C., at
the time of her death, but pressure increased to create such a
gallery with the help of President Theodore Roosevelt, who
campaigned for one in 1904, but Congress failed to act on his
request. In 1905, the District of Columbia Supreme Court ruled
that the Smithsonian collection fell within the description of "A
National Gallery of Art," and as a result, her collection was
delivered to the Smithsonian in 1906. The Lane bequest
reawakened the Smithsonian Institution's interest in art, and it
was known as the National Gallery of Art until 1937, when the
name was changed to the Smithsonian American Art Museum,
as it remains today.[97]

The bulk of the Smithsonian National Gallery of Art
consisted of Lane's collection and the William T. Evans collection
of contemporary American art (added in 1907 with President
Theodore Roosevelt's influence). The new additions greatly

expanded the Smithsonian's holdings and further encouraged bequests such as theirs.

For the next 12 years though, the third largest of Lane's bequests caused an even larger controversy than the 29 or so articles she left to the Corcoran. It would arouse sentiments that had been buried for more than half a century, yet it had not even been built.

Chapter 14
All She Wanted
Was a Monument

If in 15 years it had not happened, it probably was not going to happen, and it almost did not happen.

On Page 5 of the December 19, 1917, edition of *The Washington Post*, the headline read "$100,000 Statue of Buchanan Lost to City Unless Congress Soon Acts — Provided Under the Will of Mrs. Harriet Lane Johnston, Fifteen Years' Effort Failed to Obtain Site from House and Senate — Time Limit Expires Soon."[98]

As stated in Harriet Lane Johnston's will:

> To William A. Fisher of the City of Baltimore, Calderon Carlisle and E, Francis Riggs of the City of Washington, and Lawrason Riggs of the City of Baltimore, and the survivors and survivor of them, his executors, administrators and assigns, I give and bequeath the sum of one hundred thousand (100,000) dollars to be known as the "James Buchanan Monument Fund" in trust to hold the same and keep the same invested until disposed of as hereinafter provided, that is to say:[99]
>
> * * *
>
> To secure from the Congress of the United States the designation of a suitable site in the City of Washington to be approved and accepted by them, the trustees aforesaid, and the permission and consent of Congress to erect on said site a statue in bronze or marble of my uncle James Buchanan the said statue to be paid for by my said trustees

out of the fund hereinbefore provided. And the said trustees are hereby authorized forthwith to procure proper designs or models for said statue with a view to the selection of a suitable design and the submission of the same to Congress in connection with their application for the necessary authority and permission in regard to the site. And I direct that on the pedestal of the statue the trustees aforesaid shall place, in addition to other appropriate inscriptions, the noble and truthful words applied to my uncle by the Honorable Jeremiah S. Black [Buchanan's Secretary of State] "The incorruptible statesman whose walk was upon the mountain ranges of the law."[100]

If any of the said fund or the increment thereof shall remain after discharging the trusts aforesaid then the same shall be paid over to the Harriet Lane Home for Invalid Children of Baltimore City, the residuary legatee hereinafter named. And if my said trustees shall not be able within fifteen years from the date of my death [July 3, 1918] ... to get the permission or the consent of Congress to place said statue on an appropriate site in the City of Washington to be approved and accepted by my said trustees, then the whole of the said sum of one hundred thousand (100,000.) dollars, with its increment, or such part as shall not have been expended in the discharge of the trusts hereinbefore set out, or any part of them, is to be paid over to the Harriet Lane Home for Invalid Children of the City of Baltimore.[101]

She provided the money, so what was the problem? Although Lane was still the most admired woman in Washington and well-regarded by all who remembered her, "Nunc" was not. Forty-nine years after his death, and President James Buchanan was still a polarizing figure, and the congressmen who were "trashing" his legacy were all born after he served as President!

By 1917, the Fine Arts Commission had approved a site in Meridian Hill Park, and a Baltimore sculptor, Hans Schuler, had completed a design.[102] But Congress blamed Lane for "unwittingly [adding] complications by testamentary stipulations that the pedestal of her uncle's statue should bear as an inscription, 'the noble and truthful words.'"[103] Representative Clarence Benjamin Miller (R-Minn.) blocked the resolution and said, "I would like to have someone tell me, if he can, what distinguished services Buchanan rendered anybody that will justify erecting a monument costing the enormous sum of $100,000 to be paid for by anybody. ... It seems not the best time in the world for us to authorize the building of a monument to an ex-President ... and I say this with all sincerity, who has perhaps little other than that he once was President, to commend him to our consideration." Did they not remember Buchanan's public service to his country for over four decades or the fact that Abraham Lincoln carried on Buchanan's policies until Fort Sumter was attacked? For that matter, what memorable things had Miller done? A search for the honorable Mr. Miller reveals only that he died in 1922 and was buried soon after.[104]

Democratic House Leader, Claude Kitchin (D-N.C.), announced a program of legislation that eliminated practically everything except appropriations bills, other war measures, and women's suffrage from consideration during the session that would commence in January 1918. However, Chairman James Luther Slayden (D-Tex.) of the House Library Committee was determined to have the Buchanan legislation up for a vote immediately after the holiday recess.[105] Representative Joseph Walsh (R-Mass.) declared on February 13 that a comparison of Buchanan to Lincoln "bordered on blasphemy." During that same debate, Representative Irvine Luther Lenroot (R-Wisc.) declared that Buchanan's actions were almost traitorous and said, "The best thing we can do for Mr. Buchanan is forget him." However, the late Buchanan had his allies in Representatives Slayden, Arthur Granville Dewalt (D-Penn.), Henry Joseph Steele (D-Penn.), and John Charles Linthicum (D-Md.).[106] Representative Joseph Hampton Moore (D-Penn.) took the floor saying, "For my part, I do not think it wise policy for the Congress of the United States under the most provoking circumstances to place the stamp of its disapproval upon a former President." General Issac R. Sherwood (D-Ohio), yelled from his seat, "I will vote for this bill!" With his arm in a sling as he was recovering from a recent fall, Joseph Gurney "Uncle Joe" Cannon (D-Ill.) strode to the front of the House and closed the debate with, "Let us forget, in God's name let the dead past bury its dead," which brought the Democratic side to its feet.[107]

In a February 15 letter to the editor of *The Washington Post*, Mary F. Henderson, wrote:

> There seems to be a misunderstanding about the placing of the Buchanan statue in Meridian Hill Park. The plan is not to place this comparatively small, sitting figure of Buchanan at the crest of the hill, but at the bottom of the hill at the corner of Florida Avenue and Fifteenth Street. The general plan calls for landscape features covering 100 by 400 feet of ground bordering on Florida Avenue — all to be paid for by this Harriet Lane Johnston Fund. ... Our country is indebted to Harriet Lane Johnston for her very valuable art collection willed to his city and which marks the opening of our National Art Gallery. It is most unfortunate to have her second gift to the city so scorned.[108]

The bill eventually passed in the House, but Senator Reed Smoot (R-Utah) prevented consideration in the Senate on March 19, after Senator Philander Chase Knox (D-Penn.) brought the resolution up for a vote. Perhaps Smoot was still bitter about Buchanan for preventing Brigham Young from establishing his own Mormon nation in Utah, where the Bachelor President remained and still is a vilified figure.[109] Ask any Mormon missionary about President James Buchanan, and one will get an earful.

On June 14, Senator Henry Cabot Lodge (R-Mass.) declared Buchanan disloyal and compared him to Benedict Arnold and further said the statue would honor a President "upon whom rests the shadow of disloyalty in the great office to which he was elected." Lodge went further to complain that Buchanan did not deserve a statue when there were none in the capital to John Adams, Thomas Jefferson or James Madison. Senator John Walter Smith (D-Md.) shot back that the Senate should not deny Harriet Lane Johnston the opportunity to pay this last act of affection to her uncle. Lodge, quick with a response said, "Benedict Arnold retained the love of his wife and the affection of his children, but I think it is hardly an argument for erecting a statue in his memory in Washington."[110] Fortunately for Buchanan, the Democrats were in the majority.

The Buchanan Statue was approved by an Act of Congress, June 27, 1918 (40 Stat. 632).[111] President Woodrow Wilson, a Democrat, signed the bill authorizing the erection of the James Buchanan Statue in Meridian Hill Park on the same day, which was six days before the July 3, 1918, deadline.

With that, America's First Lady had the final word on America's Bachelor President.

Meridian Hill Park was so named because it is a 12-acre site situated on a near perfect north-south axis and is located in Northwest Washington, D.C. The park is bordered by 16th, Euclid, 15th, and W Streets. John Porter built a mansion on the site called "Meridian Hill," which was on the exact longitude of the original District of Columbia milestone marker that was set down on April 15, 1791, at Jones Point, Va. The marker was placed by Major Andrew Ellicott, who was assisted by Benjamin Banneker, the "Sable Astronomer."

Banneker was born in 1731 in Maryland, the son of a former slave. Banneker started studying astronomy when he was 58, and he was soon after able to predict future solar and lunar eclipses. He compiled the ephemeris, or information table, that was used in annual almanacs that were published from 1792 to 1797. "Benjamin Banneker's Almanac" was sold in Pennsylvania, Virginia and Kentucky. In 1791, Banneker was assigned the technical assistant in the calculating and surveying of the Federal District, the former Foggy Bottom, Maryland, now known as Washington, D.C. George Washington had chosen the site for the new capital city, which was a compromise between Alexander Hamilton and Thomas Jefferson for the North needed the South's wealth to pay off Revolutionary War debts, hence the capital city being located in the South. The original plans for the Federal City were destroyed in a fire and if not for Benjamin Banneker's extraordinary memory, the traffic circles in Washington, D.C., would be easier to navigate today.

John Quincy Adams moved into Porter's Mansion, located in the park, when his term as president ended in 1829, when all of the high ground surrounding the park was known as "Meridian Hill." Therefore, he was the first president to reside in Washington post-presidency and not Woodrow Wilson, who lived in Washington until he died in 1924. In 1830 and without his knowledge, Adams was elected to the House of Representatives by his home district of Plymouth,

Massachusetts. He served in the Congress until he collapsed on the floor of the House of Representatives and died in 1848, when James Buchanan was Secretary of State during President Polk's administration.

Prior to the Civil War, the area became a pleasure park for the surrounding neighborhoods, and during the war, Union troops used it as an encampment. The U.S. government purchased the present day park in 1910, which was managed by the Office of Public Buildings and Grounds. In 1914, the Department of the Interior hired landscape architect George Burnap to design a formal park. The idea was to model it after the Renaissance and Italian gardens popular in many world capitals. Burnap's designs were revised by landscape architect Horace Peaslee, under the direction of the Fine Arts Commission of Washington, D.C. Park construction began in 1914 and was completed in 1936. In 1933, the grounds were transferred to the National Park Service.

As Mary F. Henderson stated, it is in the southeast corner of Meridian Hill Park (Florida Avenue and 15th Street NW) that the only monument to President James Buchanan in Washington, D.C., is located. The monument consists of a bronze statue of a seated Buchanan on a platform of granite. On either side of the statue are two figures representing Law and Diplomacy. Etched into the monument on the right side is the statement by Jeremiah S. Black, "The Incorruptible Statesman Whose Walk Was Upon the Mountain Ranges of the Law," and on left side is the statement, "James Buchanan of Pennsylvania, President of the United States, MDCCCIVII MDCCCLXI."

"Before a distinguished group of government officials, diplomats and Pennsylvanians gathered in Meridian Hill Park"[112] on June 26, 1930, President Herbert Hoover presided over the dedication of the statue of President James Buchanan, one hundred years after the birth of America's First Lady. The statue was officially presented to the American people by former ambassador to Japan, Roland S. Morris, who represented Pennsylvania Governor John S. Fisher. Senior Pietro Gladiatore Gentile, vocalist of the Los Angeles Post of the American Legion, sang the Star Spangled Banner and a detachment from the headquarters company of the U.S. Army presented arms while the bachelor chief executive's cousin, Mrs. Francis H. Denny, did the honors of unveiling the memorial.[113]

A dozen carrier pigeons were released, while Morris declared, "that Buchanan had faced unexpected and bewildering difficulties and the failure of his administration merely justified his mediation policies. There were years when few dared speak well of Buchanan, but as the heat of passions died, his qualities as a statesman became apparent, and we now recognize him as a truly great man. His chief objective was the preservation of the Union by peaceful means, but he was opposed by people incapable of being conciliated, and the frustrations of his plans in no way reflects upon his principles or his ability. Throughout his long and distinguished public life he held that calm reasoning and mediation were the chief requisites for statesmanship."[114]

With that, Hoover, the thirty-first President of the United States, delivered the following address:[115]

Remarks at the Dedication of a Statue of James Buchanan by President Herbert Hoover

My fellow countrymen:

It is my pleasant duty today to take part in the formal dedication of this statue of the fifteenth President of the United States. These memorials of the past not only pay honor to the virtues of the men who have held the highest office which our citizens can bestow, but they also help to fix in our minds the orderly march of our life as a nation.

James Buchanan, whom we honor here today, occupied the Presidency at a moment when no human power could have stayed the inexorable advance of a great national conflict. The black clouds of dissension had gathered over the country when he entered upon his duties. The thunderbolts of war were withheld until he left the scene, but throughout his administration the sky was clouded with the ominous threatenings of storm.

He had shared in the notable efforts to solve the problem of slavery by compromise. His partners in these efforts were the ablest and most penetrating minds of his day, and it was largely by chance that his Presidency coincided with the ultimate failure of these hopes. He was the last outstanding figure surviving of one of the most remarkable groups of men in our history, and it was his fate to represent them at the moment when they must yield to younger men representing a more aggressive conception of the Nation's duty. He played his part with a dignity and courage that only now are receiving the recognition they deserve.

Mr. Buchanan served his country during a long and active life — as a Senator of prominence and as a diplomat. His first great diplomatic success was in negotiating our first commercial treaty with Russia. He performed important services as Ambassador to London. As Secretary of State under President Polk, he skillfully guided our position with respect to the Oregon boundary and settled this delicate question advantageously and peacefully. Both as negotiator while Ambassador and as director of policies while Secretary of State, Mr. Buchanan established for himself one of the most eminent reputations in these fields in all our history.

His career was rich in achievements deserving the gratitude of his country. But its most appealing side should also be mentioned here. A bachelor, and engrossed in public and private business, he found time to rear and educate an orphaned niece in a manner that would have done credit to any father. His wise and affectionate letters to Harriet Lane are a charming addition to American literature, and are still to be read with pleasure. It is due to Miss Lane's devoted appreciation of his kindness that this statue has been erected, for she left provisions for it in her will. This is, therefore, an occasion not only honoring a great patriot but also testifying to a real filial affection.

I now dedicate the statue of James Buchanan, fifteenth President of the United States, to the people of this country, for a memorial of his services as a man and as a chief officer of Government."

Even in death, with her signature dignity and grace, America's First Lady had vindicated her favorite uncle. More importantly, she had established an everlasting legacy for herself as well.

The Inaugural Gown
26-year-old Harriet Lane

The Archives and Special Collections, Wadner-Spahr Library,
Dickinson College, Carlisle, Pennsylvania

Inaugural Ball, Judiciary Square, Washington, D.C. (March 4, 1857)

Library of Congress

First Inauguration to be Photographed (March 4, 1857)

Library of Congress

28-year-old Harriet Lane (1858)

James Buchanan Foundation for the Preservation of Wheatland

30-year-old Harriet Lane (1860)

James Buchanan Foundation for the Preservation of Wheatland

40-year-old Harriet Lane (1870)

James Buchanan Foundation for the Preservation of Wheatland

40-year-old Harriet Lane (1870)

James Buchanan Foundation for the Preservation of Wheatland

50-year-old Harriet Lane (1880)

Smithsonian American Art Museum

68-year-old Harriet Lane (1898)

St. Albans School, Washington, D.C.

69-year-old Harriet Lane (1899)

Smithsonian American Art Museum

65-year-old James Buchanan (1856)

James Buchanan Foundation for the Preservation of Wheatland

69-year-old James Buchanan (1860)

James Buchanan Foundation for the Preservation of Wheatland

30-year-old Lily Macalester (1860)

Mount Vernon Ladies' Association

50-year-old Lily Macalester (1880)

Mount Vernon Ladies' Association

18-year-old Prince of Wales (1860)

Library of Congress

64-year-old William Rufus Devane King (1850)

Library of Congress

USRMCS Harriet Lane (1857)

United States Navy

United States Coast Guard Medium Endurance Cutter (WMEC) 903 Harriet Lane (1984)

United States Coast Guard

James Buchanan's Wheatland
Front View

Back View

Milton Stern (10/03)

James Buchanan's Grave

Milton Stern (10/03)

White House and Surrounding Neighborhoods (1904)

Library of Congress

**Harriet Lane's Two Washington Residences
(just blocks from the White House)
1737 I Street (circled left)
1730 K Street (circled right)**

1737 I Street Residence

The Washington Post (1930)

Her Misspelled Name in the City Directory

CAUTION—The buying public will please not con
ound the SOHMER Piano with one of a similar
ounding name of a cheap grade. Our name spells
S-O-H-M-E-R.
ON SALE ONLY AT HUGO WORCH, 923 F St. N. W.

567	JOH
nw	Johnson Guy H, lawyer, 500 5th nw, h 1706 9th nw
e	Johnson G V, police, 505 12th nw
al	Johnson Hannah, wid Anderson, 612 K sw
	Johnson Hannah F, domestic, 209 Ball al nw
th	Johnson Hannah M, teacher, 5 Grant pl nw
	Johnson Hannah P, teacher, 12 Grant pl nw
	Johnson Hanson, lab, 810 13th ne
w	Johnson Harrie, dom, 1343 Cedar al nw
v	Johnson Harriet Lane, 1737 I nw
w	Johnson Harrison, lab, 2232 Cleveland av nw
—	Johnson Harry, bkkpr, 1501 7th nw
—	Johnson Harry, huckster, 417 1st sw
	Johnson Harry, lab, 28 5th ne
	Johnson Harry, lab, 631 I sw

BOYD'S DIR

Kiplinger Library of the City Museum of Washington, D.C.

Lane-Johnston Building and Cornerstone, St. Albans School, Washington, D.C.

Milton Stern (02/05)

James Buchanan Monument, Meridian Hill Park, Washington, D.C.

Milton Stern (02/05)

The Final Resting Place of
Harriet Lane Johnston,
Henry Elliot Johnston,
James Buchanan Johnston, and Henry
Elliot Johnston, Jr.
Greenmount Cemetery, Baltimore

Milton Stern (05/04)

Annex A
The Effects of United States History on Harriet Lane's Seating Arrangements

Toward the end of James Buchanan's only term as President of the United States (1857–1861), the country was on the brink of civil war. As a result, First Lady Harriet Lane used her diplomatic skills to their fullest to arrange the seating at White House dinners. She was not going to be responsible for any brawls during dessert! So, to get a complete grasp of Washington politics prior to 1856, one must have an understanding of American history from 1787 (the year the Constitution was adopted) to 1861 (the year the Civil War began).

From the beginning, the majority of the framers of the Constitution did not want to tackle the issue of slavery. All of them knew the irony of a nation founded on the principles of freedom and democracy embracing the institution of slavery, but to them, there was one issue of higher importance — the formation of a more perfect Union. The Southern states where slavery was most prevalent and where the economy was believed to be most dependent on slavery (slavery was legal in many of the northern states at the time) were also among the most prosperous and populous of the original thirteen. Therefore, whatever was needed to ensure their staying in the Union was done, and the slavery issue was left for the states to decide. From 1820 to 1861, more than at any other time, slavery would be at the forefront of American politics.

By 1820, when President James Monroe was serving the third year in his first term, the United States was a divided nation. Free states in the North, and slave states in the South (slavery also was legal in the District of Columbia). Until July 15, 1870, with the readmission of Georgia into the Union, the President of the United States was the chief executive of a country split by the impact of slavery.

With the Louisiana Purchase of 1803, which doubled the size of the United States, and Spain's agreement to cede Florida in 1819, slavery would remain on the front burner as new territories were established and new states would petition for entrance into the Union. Thus, a series of compromises and Supreme Court decisions would attempt to allay the fears on both sides about slavery's expansion and limitation.

America's Time Line (1786–1861)

September 9, 1786. George Washington, a slave owner, calls for the abolition of slavery before the Constitution is written or adopted. In his will, Washington frees his slaves (to be effective upon the death of Martha Washington).

February 1793. Fugitive Slave Law. "No state shall protect in their respective states: criminal fugitives, servants, or slaves. The state must apprehend, secure, and deliver to the state or states criminals, servants, or slaves."

January 1808. The African slave trade and the importation of slaves from Africa is outlawed by both the United States and England. It will remain legal in Cuba until the 1870s. England will outlaw slavery at home and in all British colonies in 1833.

March 1820: Missouri Compromise. Maine, formerly a part of Massachusetts, is admitted to the United States as a free state, and Missouri is admitted as a slave state. With the exception of Missouri, slavery is prohibited in the territories derived from the Louisiana Purchase north of latitude 36°30'.

The following states are admitted under the Missouri Compromise:

1836, Arkansas, slave
1837, Michigan, free
1845, Florida, slave
1845, Texas, slave
1846, Iowa, free
1846, Wisconsin, free

December 1823: The Monroe Doctrine. President James Monroe declares that American continents are hereby off limits for further colonization by any European powers (Secretary of State John Quincy Adams is instrumental in drafting *The Monroe Doctrine*).

March 1824: Gibbons v. Ogen. This case, although not directly related to slavery, defines Congress's right to regulate interstate commerce. Slaves, which are considered property, fall under these regulations.

March 4, 1825. President John Quincy Adams is inaugurated. Although not as vocal while in the White House, Adams, while serving in the House of Representatives post presidency, is an outspoken critic of the Congressional gag rule on abolitionist petitions being introduced in the House. Buchanan will chair the Committee on Abolitionist Petitions during his time in the Senate (1836-45). Of the first six presidents, Adams and his father, are the only non-slave owners and the only ones not re-elected to a second term.

May 1830. Indian Removal Act. This act authorizes the forced removal of American Indians living east of the Mississippi River to the West. Almost 50,000 American Indians are relocated by the late 1830s. In 1838, more than 4,000 die among the 15,000 American Indians along the Trail of Tears from Georgia to present-day Oklahoma. Although not directly related to slavery, this act portends racist American policies that will persist until the Civil Rights Act of 1964. Harriet Lane is born on May 9, 1830, and as First Lady, she will be an advocate for improving the plight of the American Indians, earning her the title "Great Mother of the Indians."

April 1836. Texas defeats Mexico at San Jacinto and declares its independence. Texas is annexed by the United States and on March 1, 1845, is admitted as a slave state (Mexico had already outlawed slavery in 1829).

July 1845. Manifest Destiny. The term is first used in a magazine article by John L. O'Sullivan. Manifest Destiny represents the belief by white Americans that the United States is destined to expand across the continent (some believed beyond the continent). Buchanan uses this doctrine while Minister to Great Britain to argue for the annexation of Cuba through the *Ostend Manifesto.* For the remainder of his political career, Buchanan continues to urge the government to annex Cuba even though abolitionist fear the annexation of Cuba will only expand slavery.

1846–1848. The Mexican War. Abraham Lincoln, while serving his only term in the House of Representatives, declares the Mexican War, "Polk's War." The war ends with the signing of the Treaty of Guadalupe Hidalgo, in which Secretary of State James Buchanan is instrumental. Through the terms of the treaty, the Rio Grande becomes the official southern boundary of Texas, and for $15,000,000, the United States purchases the territories that will become California, Nevada, Utah, most of New Mexico and Arizona, and parts of Colorado and Wyoming. Slavery will be a hot button issue in the admission of some of these territories as states. Although not related to slavery, the Utah Territory will be the first territory to try to stage a rebellion against the United States government under the leadership of Brigham Young in 1857, while Buchanan is president. To this day, Buchanan is still vilified in parts of Utah for quashing Young's rebellion.

July 1848. Women's Rights Convention, Seneca Falls, New York. Among the issues discussed is the abolition of slavery.

July 1850. President Taylor dies. Millard Fillmore becomes the second vice president to ascend to the presidency and the last Whig to serve as president. Fillmore, in 1843, rents a room at Ms. Pittman's boarding house, located on 3rd Street between Pennsylvania Avenue and C Streets in Washington. Buchanan also boards there at the time. Fillmore will run against Buchanan in 1856 on the Free Soil Party ticket.

September 1850. The Compromise of 1850. In the last true effort to preserve the Union, Senator Henry Clay proposes and Congress passes five acts called the Compromise of 1850. Although passed with the hopes of quieting the controversies, it does more to destroy the Union than any other effort before it. The five acts are:

1. The federal government is allowed to enforce the fugitive slave laws, which up to this point are enforced by the states with free states mostly ignoring them. The compromise says that any slaves escaping from the South to freedom in the North shall be returned to their masters. Bounty hunters receive a bounty for each slave they return. Some free black people are captured by bounty hunters and sold as slaves. Any person who does not help a bounty hunter can be punished under the law. The Underground Railroad expands, and many slaves escape to Canada.

2. The entire territory of California is admitted as one free state.

3 and 4. New Mexico and Utah decide within their territories and by their residents whether to be admitted as slave or free states.

5. The slave trade in the District of Columbia is outlawed although it is still legal to own slaves in the nation's capital.

December 30, 1853. Gadsen Purchase Treaty. President Franklin Pierce signs this treaty, which for $10,000,000 acquires border territory from Mexico, which completes present day Arizona and New Mexico. James Buchanan is serving as Minister to the Court of St. James at the time and relays the news of the Gadsen Purchase to the British, who are always concerned with American territorial expansion.

May 1854. Kansas-Nebraska Act. This act establishes the territories of Kansas and Nebraska, and as a result nullifies the Missouri Compromise of 1820. Kansas attempts to be admitted as a slave state under the Lecompton Constitution with President Buchanan's support.

March 6, 1857. Dred Scott. President James Buchanan is inaugurated on March 4, and two days later, the Supreme Court hands down the *Dred Scott* decision, which holds that slaves are property and not citizens of the United States. It continues that slaves are not freed by the mere fact that they stepped on the soil of a free state.

December 20, 1860, South Carolina secedes from the United States, which is not surprising as South Carolina has often times threatened to secede since as far back as 1833. By the time of Lincoln's Inauguration on March 4, 1861, the following states secede from the union: Mississippi (January 9, 1861), Florida (January 10, 1861), Alabama (January 11, 1861), Georgia (January 19, 1861), Louisiana (January 26, 1861), and Texas (February 1, 1861), giving the Confederacy seven states in its union. By the end of the May 1861, the following states join their cause: Virginia (April 17, 1861), Arkansas (May 6, 1861), Tennessee (May 7, 1861), and North Carolina (May 21, 1861), making them eleven strong, leaving 22 states in the North.

January 29, 1861, Kansas is admitted as a free state by the newly elected Republican Congress.

Harriet Lane Johnston's Will

LAST WILL AND TESTAMENT AND CODICILS OF
HARRIET LANE JOHNSTON

JOSIAH LEE JOHNSTON
D.K. ESTE FISHER
WM. Q. .JOHNSON
MAY S. KENNEDY
EXECUTORS AND EXECUTRIX

I, Harriet Lane Johnston, of the City of Baltimore, State of Maryland, widow of Henry E. Johnston, late of said City and State, being of sound and disposing mind, memory and understanding, do make, publish and declare this my last will and testament .in manner and form following, that is to say:

After the payment of all my just debts, funeral expenses and the costs and expenses of administering upon my estate, I give, bequeath and devise my entire estate and property, real and personal, legal or equitable, in possession or expectant, which I now own or in which I have any estate or interest, and all which I may hereafter acquire or in which I may hereafter have any estate or interest legally susceptible of disposition by will or testament, including all the property, real or personal, of any description of my late husband over which I have the power of disposition, by will or testament, in the following manner that is to say:

To Josiah Lee Johnston, my husband's brother, I give and bequeath all of my household linen in which the Johnston coat of arms is woven or on which it is embroidered or otherwise displayed, and I also give and bequeath to him the watches and chains belonging to my said husband and to my son James Buchanan Johnston. And also to the end that they may be by him distributed, in his discretion, among my said husband's friends and relatives, all the scarf-pins and other jewelry and personal ornaments which belonged to my said husband; and I direct that he shall distribute to Mary C. Speer and Charles E. Speer, each, a handsome scarf-pin, as such was my husband's wish.

To my nephews John N. Lane, James Buchanan Lane and Elliott Eskridge Lane, I give and bequeath all my gold pens and pencils and all the old-time jewelry which belonged to my mother, and also all the silver-ware and set of pink china without the laurel border and the set of white and gilt china which I got from my father, mother and sister and my uncle James Buchanan, and I also give to them my mother's embroidery pictures and the small likenesses of my father and my uncles John and Thomas Lane and three photographs of my uncle James Buchanan; also the chair and walking sticks and canes of my uncle James Buchanan and the mahogany furniture from Wheatland and the eleven pictures of the Royal family given me by the Prince of Wales.

To John N. Lane, my said nephew, give and bequeath my seal ring with the Lane crest; to James Buchanan Lane, my said nephew, the portrait of my mother and my grand-father Buchanan's eight day clock; to Elliott Eskridge Lane, my said nephew, the miniatures of my brother Eskridge and my sister Mary and my emerald and diamond ring with cameo of President Buchanan; to Patty Jenkins Lane, my niece, my cameo bracelet with uncle James Buchanan's hair in it, my diamond lily of the valley brooch, my sister's cluster diamond ring, my long pearl earrings and the large chair of my own work.

To Josiah Lee Johnston, my husband's brother, Mary W. Johnston and Bessie E. Gresham, my husband's two sisters, and to Emily Johnston Hoffman, my husband's niece, I give and bequeath all my silver-ware which came to me from my husband's mother's estate. I give and bequeath to Margaret P. Johnston my large pearl earrings; I give and bequeath to Emily Johnston Hoffman my ring of six diamond bands, gold spoon which belonged to my son James Buchanan Johnston, silver bowl in which my son Harry was baptized, my cameo and diamond locket with her grandfather's hair, silver pap-bowl, plate and spoon from "Cousin Katie," gold locket with large pearl, containing my husband's likeness and my son James Buchanan Johnston's gold clasp.

To Mary C. Speer I give and bequeath my ruby and diamond ring and my large diamond pendant and little Harry's foot-rest; also my set of pink china with laurel bonier and the Johnston coat of arms; to Ettie W. Speer my diamond heart, and to Louise Speer my brooch with five pearls and diamonds and diamond and emerald ring.

To L. Waterbury Johnston, eldest son of Elliott Johnston, I give and bequeath my son Harry's watch and chain; if L. Waterbury Johnston does not survive me then to his brother Elliot; both watch and chain belonged to their grandfather.

To Joseph N. Henry, son of James Buchanan Henry, I give and bequeath my earrings and brooch of small pearls which belonged to his mother.

To Mrs. Herman J. Groesbeck, of Cincinnati, I give and bequeath my diamond and blue enameled bracelet and horse-shoe locket and chain.

To May S. Kennedy and Mary C. Speer, and the survivor of them/I give and bequeath the bust of myself.

To May S. Kennedy, my cousin, I give and bequeath my onyx and diamond brooch and buttons with monogram H.R.L. thereon, my solitaire diamond ring, my prie Dieu, square stool of my own work, my rosewood furniture, wardrobe, dressing table and accessories, used by me in my youth, all my wearing apparel, my sapphire and diamond ring and the miniature of myself by Brown, which miniature and ring last mentioned she is to have for her life and after her death I give and bequeath the said miniature and ring last mentioned to my niece Patty Jenkins Lane.

To the eldest daughter of Judge Robert Gilmer I give and bequeath my locket containing a lock of her mother's hair.

To Mrs. F. W. Brune I give and bequeath my prayer-books, studs and other articles I received from my cousins William and Carrie Johnston; to Mary G. Shapter; of 7 Clarendon Place, Hyde Park Garden, London, England, my round brooch, pearl center and enameled in green containing her mother's hair, and also my diamond crescent.

To Mrs. Horace Riddle I give and bequeath my blue enameled and pearl ring and pearl brooch containing lock of my sister's hair.

To Kate W. Riddle I give and bequeath my set of amethyst and pearls, consisting of brooch, earrings, bracelet, buttons and ring with diamonds, and small chair of my own work.

To Rebecca Black Hornsby I give and bequeath my opal and diamond ring, and a photograph of my uncle President James Buchanan.

To the Regent and Ladies of the Mount Vernon Association, to be placed and kept in the Mansion House of General Washington at Mount Vernon, I give and bequeath the painting by Rossiter of the visit of my uncle, President Buchanan, and the Prince of Wales, to Mount Vernon.

To the Trustees of the Corcoran Gallery of Art, to be placed and kept in the Art Gallery, I give and bequeath the miniature by Brown of President Buchanan, the portrait of the Prince of Wales, and the first Atlantic cable message sent to this country as it was received by my uncle James Buchanan, now framed and hanging in my house.

To the United States of America, to be placed and kept in the Executive Mansion, I give and bequeath the bust of President Buchanan and the portrait of him painted before his going to Russia as Minister of the United States to that country. The portrait was considered to be the best likeness of him ever taken and I venture to express the wish that this portrait may be substituted for any portrait which may be in the Executive Mansion at the time this bequest takes effect.

To the Peabody Institute of Baltimore I give and bequeath the bust of my said husband, Henry E. Johnston, and the statue of my son Harry by Rhinehart to be placed and kept in the Rhinehart collection of that institution.

To the Vestry of St. Paul's Episcopal Church, Baltimore, I give and bequeath my pair of silver candelabra upon condition that they accept them as they are to be placed and used upon the altar of said Church, inscribing them with an appropriate inscription; otherwise I give the one of the said candelabra, which came from his mother's estate to Josiah Lee Johnston, and the other one, which my husband had made afterwards to match the original, I give and bequeath to Mary C. Speer for her life and then to Patty Jenkins Lane.

To the Harriet Lane Home for Invalid Children of Baltimore City I give and bequeath the portrait in oil of my said husband Henry E. Johnston in his youth, the portrait of my son Buchanan by Pennington; also the three pictures over my mantel-piece, the colored photographs of my children and other articles connected with them to be placed in a room in said Home set apart for the reception and custody of said articles, and I also give and bequeath to said Home all my bed and table linen, pictures, books and furniture which may be suitable for its uses and purposes and not hereinbefore or hereinafter bequeathed otherwise. It is my desire that my cousin May S. Kennedy shall select what may be suitable for and useful for the Home and to this end I suggest that she should seek the assistance of Katharine W. Riddle and Mary C. Speer, and I direct that Mary C. Speer and Katharine W. Riddle, or the survivor, should perform the office if May S. Kennedy shall not survive me.

To my cousin, May S. Kennedy, I give and bequeath all of my household furniture, books, papers, pictures, linen, silver, household ornaments, jewels and other personal ornaments, not hereinbefore or hereinafter specifically bequeathed, to be by her distributed in such manner as I may by memorandum in writing addressed to her, direct, and in default of any such memorandum being found after my death to distribute as she thinks I would wish, and, in the absence of any knowledge of my wishes, to keep for herself. And in order that the distribution of said articles may be made without removal I direct that my dwelling house be kept open for sufficient time, not exceeding one year after my death, at the expense of my estate, with the articles aforesaid therein, and the distribution thereof to be made therefrom; and during this time or so much thereof as may be necessary my said cousin shall have the privilege of residing in my house.

Should the said May S. Kennedy not survive me, then I give and bequeath the said articles upon the same terms and conditions in all respects to Mary C. Speer and should she not survive me, then upon the same terms and conditions in all respects to Kate W. Riddle.

Should all three of said legatees die before me then I give and bequeath the same to my executors hereinafter named, upon the same terms and conditions, except that in case I fail to leave any memorandum in writing directing the distribution thereof, my executors will dispose of the same at private sale and the proceeds thereof shall thereupon become and be treated as a part of the general residue of my estate and be applied as hereinafter directed as to said general residue.

Should any of the persons to whom I have given specific legacies by this will die before me, then I direct that such specific legacies shall fall into and become part of the preceding residuary bequest to May S. Kennedy and follow the disposition thereof.

To the Vestry of St. Paul's Parish in the City of Baltimore, I give and bequeath the sum of two thousand (2000.) dollars in trust to invest the same and out of the income to keep in order the memorial window to my two sons, and the residue, if any, of said income, in any year to apply for the benefit of the poor of said Parish.

To the Vestry of St. John's Church of Waverly, Baltimore County, Maryland, I give and bequeath one thousand (1000.) dollars in trust for the benefit of the orphanage of the said parish.

To Miss Gale, otherwise called Sister Anna Maria, in charge of St. John's Orphanage at Waverly in Baltimore County, I give and bequeath one thousand (1000.) dollars for life and after her death the said sum is to fall into and become part of the general residuum of my estate and follow the disposition thereof.

To the St. John's Orphanage of Washington, D.C., I give and bequeath the sum of one thousand dollars.

To the Johns Hopkins University of the City of Baltimore, in the State of Maryland, I give and bequeath the sum of Sixty thousand (60000.) dollars upon trust to found and perpetually to maintain in said University three free scholarships to be called respectively the "Henry E. Johnston" the "James Buchanan Johnston" and the "Henry E. Johnston Jr." scholarships, to be awarded to poor youths under such conditions as the University may establish.

To the Vestry of St. James Church, at Lancaster, Pennsylvania, I give and bequeath the sum of one thousand (1000.) dollars in trust to invest the same and out of the income to keep in good order condition and repair the memorial window to my son Buchanan, and the tablet in memory of my husband and my son Harry, and the balance of the said net income, if any, in any year, to apply to the Parish uses.

To the Woman's Hospital of Baltimore, Maryland, I give and bequeath the sum of one thousand (1000.) dollars.

To the Woodward Hill Cemetery Company of Lancaster, Pennsylvania, or to the corporation, by whatsoever name known, or to whoever may be the proprietor thereof, I give and bequeath the sum of five hundred (500.) dollars to be invested and the income therefrom to be used in keeping in order the lot in said Cemetery interred the remains of my Uncle James Buchanan and the adjoining lot in case of the purchase thereof hereinafter provided for, in preserving the monuments therein and having the grass cut at least once a mouth during the growing season. I direct my executors hereinafter named to purchase if practicable the interest of Reverend E.Y. Buchanan in the lot adjoining the one last above mentioned, and for this purpose I give and bequeath to them such sum of money as may be necessary, not exceeding the sum of two hundred and fifty (250.) dollars. And in the event of said purchase I further direct them to remove the present enclosure and enclose the two lots together with a suitable granite enclosure or such as surrounds the Reynolds lot in Lancaster Cemetery.

To the Lancaster Cemetery Company at Lancaster, Pennsylvania, or the corporation or persons by a whatever name known who may be proprietors of said Lancaster Cemetery, I give and bequeath the sum of five hundred (500.) dollars, to be invested and the income therefrom applied to keeping in order the lot in said Cemetery in which are the tombs of my sister and brother Mary Lane Baker and Elliott Eskridge Lane, my uncle John N. Lane and my cousin G. Taylor Lane, and the said tombs and in cutting the grass at least once a month in the growing season.

To the Pastor and Elders of the Presbyterian Church at Mereersburg, Pennsylvania, I give and bequeath the sum of five hundred (500) dollars, to be invested and the income therefrom to be applied in keeping in order the Buchanan and Lane lot in Waddell Cemetery near Mercersburg and in having the grass cut at least once a month in the growing season.

In case any of the above named legatees shall be incompetent in law to take or decline to accept the legacy upon the trusts therein specified for keeping in order said Cemetery lots, then I hereby direct my executors to pay over the sum or sums so declined or which cannot be excepted, to some corporation competent in law to accept and execute such trust upon the trusts as to said lots herein specified.

To each of my three nephews, John N. Lane, James N. Lane and E. Eskridge Lane, I give and bequeath the sum of twenty thousand (20000.) dollars, the aggregate of these three bequests with the preceding bequests for the benefit of members of the Lane family amounting approximately to the value of the estate, left me by my uncle James Buchanan. The increase of my separate estate having been entirely due to the care and attention of my late husband it is my wish that it should go to the Harriet Lane Home for Invalid Children of the City of Baltimore hereinafter named as residuary legatee, incorporated in my husband's lifetime and provided for in his will.

I give and bequeath to my cousin Mary C. Speer the sum of five thousand (5000.) dollars, to Kate W. Riddle one thousand (1000.) dollars, to Anna Riddle two hundred and fifty (250.) dollars, to Nannie Selden two hundred and fifty (250.) dollars; to my cousin, Julia Kennedy, five hundred (500.) dollars, to my cousin Margaret Kennedy two hundred and fifty (250) dollars; to my cousin Ethel Kennedy two hundred and fifty (250.) dollars.

To my executors I give and bequeath the sum of two thousand dollars in trust for the education of my niece Patty Jenkins Lane, if she shall not have reached the age of twenty-one years by the time of my death, but if she shall then be twenty-one years in trust to pay the same over to her absolutely.

To the Church Home Infirmary of the City of Baltimore, I give and bequeath the sum of two thousand (2000.) dollars, to be invested by it and the income applied exclusively to keeping in repair and suitably furnished the floor heretofore erected and furnished by me as a ward for boys, as a memorial of my tender regard for my deceased husband, which is known and designated as the "Henry E. Johnston Ward for Boys."

In the application of the income from the foregoing bequest it is my desire that priority be given to the Memorial Room on said flour endowed by me in memory of my children James Buchanan Johnston and Henry Elliott Johnston, Jr. the large ward and the dining room.

To Emily Johnston Hoffman, I give and bequeath for life the sum of five thousand (5000.) dollars, and after her death to her lawful children, absolutely; but if she should die without leaving any such children living at the time of her death then the said sum is go into and become part of the general residue of my estate and follow the disposition thereof.

To my executors hereinafter named I give and bequeath the sum of fifteen thousand (15000.) dollars in trust to invest the same and pay over the income therefrom to my cousin May S. Kennedy during her life and in further trust, should she in writing so request, to invest the same or any part thereof in a residence to be purchased or built for her as she may require, and to be held by said Executors in trust to permit her to use and occupy the same for life. After the death of said May S. Kennedy the said sum or any property in which it may be invested is to go to such person or persons as my said cousin May S. Kennedy may by will appoint, and in default of any such appointment to become a part of the general residue of my estate and follow the disposition thereof made herein.

I also direct my executors if his education is not completed at the time of my death to pay out of my estate the tuition and reasonable maintenance of my cousin John P. Kennedy at Stevens Institute Hoboken, New Jersey.

To my said executors I give and bequeath the sum of five thousand (5000.) dollars to be held by them in trust for the payment of the expenses of a collegiate course for whichever of the three younger sons of my nephew John N. Lane, brothers of my grand-nephew James Buchanan Lane, will faithfully prepare for and actually pursue a college course they to have the privilege of availing themselves thereof in the order of their ages, the eldest, first, and in the event of his not desiring to take advantage of it the next eldest, and so to the youngest. I also give and bequeath to my said executors the sum of five thousand (5000.)

dollars, upon the like trust for the benefit of Richard S. Lane the son of my nephew James Buchanan Lane. Should neither of the brothers of my said grand-nephew James Buchanan Lane pursue a college course as herein provided, or should the said Richard S. Lane not pursue such course, then and in both or either of said events the said sums or sum of five thousand dollars are to fall into the general residue of my estate and follow the disposition thereof.

To my servant, Eliza Butler, if in my employ at the time of my death or if she should remain in my employ until disabled from work, I give and bequeath the sum of five hundred (500.) dollars.

To William A. Fisher of the City of Baltimore, Calderon Carlisle and E. Francis Riggs of the City of Washington, and Lawrason Riggs of the City of Baltimore, and the survivors and survivor of them, his executors, administrators and assigns, I give and bequeath the sum of one hundred thousand (100000) dollars to be known as the "James Buchanan Monument Fund" in trust to hold the same and keep the same invested until disposed of as hereinafter provided, that is to say:

In Trust First. To secure for the purpose of a site for a monument, either by private negotiations or under the laws of the State of Pennsylvania, an acre or more of ground at Stony Batter, near Mercersburg. Pennsylvania, the birth place of my uncle James Buchanan, and thereon to erect a suitable monument with proper inscriptions, and I suggest as appropriate to the place and purpose of this monument a huge rock or boulder in its natural state, except that proper surfaces or tablets should be prepared or provided for necessary inscriptions, and I direct that the monument shall be surrounded by a high iron railing for its protection, but the remainder of the ground shall be left unenclosed for the free use and enjoyment of the people of the State of Pennsylvania to whose care I commit this memorial of my uncle, and upon the completion of the said monument I authorize and direct my trustees to secure the ownership of and control of said site and monument to the State of Pennsylvania to be preserved as a memorial of her distinguished citizen.

In Trust Second. To secure from the Congress of the United States the designation of a suitable site in the City of Washington to be approved and accepted by them, the trustees aforesaid, and the permission and consent of Congress to erect on said site a statue in bronze or marble of my uncle James Buchanan the said statue to be paid for by my said trustees out of the fund hereinbefore provided. And the said trustees are hereby authorized forthwith to procure proper designs or models for said statue with a view to the selection of a suitable design and the submission of the same to Congress in connection with their application for the necessary authority and permission in regard to the site. And I direct that on the pedestal of the statue the trustees aforesaid shall place, in addition to other appropriate inscriptions, the noble and truthful words applied to my uncle by the Honorable Jeremiah S. Black "The incorruptible statesman whose walk was upon the mountain ranges of the law."

In Trust Third: If any of the said fund or the increment thereof shall remain after discharging the trusts aforesaid then the same shall be paid over to the Harriet Lane Home for Invalid Children of Baltimore City, the residuary legatee hereinafter named. And if my said trustees shall not be able within fifteen years from the date of my death to secure a site at Stony Batter, or to get the permission or the consent of Congress to place said statue on an appropriate site in the City of Washington to be approved and accepted by my said trustees, then the whole of the said sum of one hundred thousand (100000.) dollars, with its increment, or such part as shall not have been expended in the discharge of the trusts hereinbefore set out, or any part of them, is to be paid over to the Harriet Lane Home for Invalid Children of the City of Baltimore.

I direct my executors to pay to the lawful authorities out of my estate any succession or other tax which maybe lawfully payable upon any of the legacies or bequests herein so that the same may not be diminished to the recipients thereof by any such taxes.

If any bequest herein made shall fail to take effect and for which event no other provision is made hereby, the same is to fall into the general residue of my estate and follow the disposition thereof.

All the general rest and residue of my property of every description which I now have or may hereafter acquire and upon which this my will can operate I give, bequeath and devise absolutely and in fee simple to my executors in and upon the following trust that is to say. If my brother-in-law Josiah Lee Johnston shall survive me and shall at any time within six calendar months after my death file in the orphans court of Baltimore City a request in writing to that effect, signed by him, then, in accordance with the intention expressed in my husband's will I direct that my executors shall pay over to him the net income from the said rest and residue of my estate for and during his life, and after his death they shall transfer, set over, deliver and convey absolutely and in fee simple to the Harriet Lane Home for Invalid Children of Baltimore City all the said rest and residue of my estate. And upon this further trust, that if the said Josiah Lee Johnston shall not within said time file such written request to my executors as aforesaid, then and in that event to transfer, set over, assign and deliver and convey to said Harriet Lane Home for Invalid Children of Baltimore City, absolutely and in fee simple all the rest and residue of my estate.

Subject to the provision aforesaid in favor of Josiah Lee Johnston I express the wish that the Harriet Lane Home for Invalid Children of Baltimore City aforesaid, may be commenced within fourteen months after my death and put in operation as soon as possible thereafter; that its benefits be not confined to children residing in the City of Baltimore only, but that they be given to white children without respect to creed, nationality or residence, and with preference in favor of boys if the income shall not suffice for all children without respect to sex, and that preference shall be given to children resident in the States of Maryland and Pennsylvania and the District of Columbia whenever the number of applicants shall make it necessary or expedient to give preference to some over others.

I request also that May S. Kennedy, Katharine W. Riddle and Mary C. Speer, if not already chosen as managers of Harriet Lane Home aforesaid, shall be added to the board as soon after my death as practicable.

I commit the selection of a site for said Home to the discretion of the corporation but earnestly recommend the selection of one where ample space may be secured and retained.

It is my desire that proper memorial tablets be placed in the buildings of said Home with suitable inscriptions to commemorate the design of the Home and connect its founder with it and to keep alive the memory of my dear husband and children.

And I charge upon the devise and bequest for its benefit that the Harriet Lane Home for Invalid Children of Baltimore City shall see that my husband's lot in Greenmount Cemetery where rests the remains of my said husband and children and will contain my own, is kept in good order and condition in accordance with the perpetual obligation assumed by said Cemetery.

And I charge upon the said devise and bequest for its benefit that the said corporation shall have the duty of keeping in good order and repair all of the monuments in the lot, and to that end I direct that on the ninth day of May in each year the manager and Sisters in charge of said Home shall proceed to said lot, inspect its condition and decorate the monuments with flowers.

I confer upon my executors power to sell any of my real estate without application to a court of equity or any orphans court, and expressly exonerate any purchaser or purchasers from my said executors from any obligation to see to the application of the purchase money.

And I authorize the trustees hereinbefore mentioned and the survivors and survivor of them and his successor or successors and my executors hereinafter named to change investments from time to time, by sale or otherwise, whenever they or he may think it advisable, and I confer upon the survivor of my executors and upon any person or persons appointed administrator or administrators cum testamento annexo of my estate the power and authority conferred in this will upon my three executors.

I hereby constitute and appoint my brother-in-law, Josiah Lee Jobnston, and William A. Fisher, both of the City of Baltimore, and

Calderon Carlisle of the City of Washington, District of Columbia, to be the executors of this my last will and testament; and I request, so far as I can control it, that no bond be required from them and the commissions to be allowed them shall be the lowest now or hereafter fixed by law.

Lastly I hereby revoke all wills and codicils by me heretofore made and declare this and none other to be my last will and testament.

In TESTIMONY WHEREOF I have hereunto set my hand and seal this first day of June 1895

HARRIET LANE JOHNSTON (SEAL)

Signed, sealed, published and declared by the above named testatrix, Harriet Lane Johnston, as and for her last will and testament, in the presence of us, who, in her presence and at her request and in the presence of each other have subscribed our names as witnesses thereto the day and year above written.

WM. G. JOHNSON,
GEO. F. APPLEBY,
OSCAR LUCKETT,

CODICIL

I, Harriet Lane Johnston, the above named testatrix, hereby make, publish and declare this as and for a codicil to my foregoing will, bearing date on the first day of June, 1895, and hereto attached.

Item First: To the corporation known as the Protestant Episcopal Cathedral Foundation of the District of Columbia, chartered by act of Congress approved January 6, 1893, I give and bequeath the sum of Two hundred thousand (200000.) dollars, in trust nevertheless for the following uses and purposes and none other, that is to say: In trust to erect a building for a school for boys to be established and maintained by said corporation, said building to be erected on land now owned or hereafter acquired by said corporation, to be known as the "Lane-Johnston" building, to the end that the family names of my husband and myself may be associated with this bequest made in loving memory of our sons provided always that no part of the said sum of Two hundred thousand (200000.) dollars is to be expended in the purchase of ground, but the whole is to be applied to the erection of such building. The said building is to be begun within six months from the time when my executors shall notify the said corporation that the fund is subject to their order and the building is to be such as will, in the opinion of those having the lawful control of the erection thereof, best promote the welfare of such school for boys, whether as the-first building erected for the establishment of such school or as an additional building for the better maintenance of such school already established. And if such corporation shall fail to begin the erection of the said "Lane-Johnston" building within the period aforesaid, whether for the establishment of such school for boys or for the better maintenance of such school already established, then it is my will that this bequest shall be void and of no effect, and the said sum of Two hundred thousand (200000.) dollars shall fall into and become a part of the residue of my estate.

Item Second: Having already taken steps to secure the collection and publication of the State Papers and correspondence of my late uncle James Buchanan, sometime President of the United States, from the beginning of his public career, with such explanatory notes, biographical and historical, as may be thought necessary to the proper appreciation of said papers and letters, and intending so far as possible in my lifetime to have this work accomplished, I nevertheless give and bequeath for this purpose the sum of Ten thousand (10000.) dollars or so much thereof as may be necessary; and I direct my executors to expend this sum or so much thereof as may be necessary for the purpose indicated on the requisition of my friend Calderon Carlisle, Esquire, of the City of Washington, District of Columbia, who at my request and in association with other gentlemen has undertaken the preliminary steps for securing this object in which I am so deeply interested. And in case said Calderon Carlisle shall not survive me then said fund, or so much thereof as may be necessary is to be disbursed according to the direction of the survivors or survivor of the gentleman acting with said Calderon Carlisle.

Item Third: I give and desire the farm in Virginia lately purchased by me, to my cousin, May S. Kennedy, for her life, with remainder to her lawful child or children, who may be living at her death, and if she shall die without leaving any child or children her surviving then and in that event the said farm is to fall into and become part of the residue of my estate. It is my will that the present tenant, Mrs. Julia Kennedy Taylor shall have the privilege of occupying the said farm under existing arrangements as long as she lives, and I direct my cousin May S. Kennedy and my executors and trustees as the case may be to respect this privilege.

There is at this time nine hundred (900.) dollars balance of purchase money due on said farm, and I have agreed to expend five hundred (500.) dollars for improvements thereon.

Item Fourth: In my bequest of my household furniture to May S. Kennedy it is provided that should she not survive me then the bequest shall be on the same terms and conditions to Mary C. Speer, and should she not survive me then to Kate W. Riddle, and in case none of the three survive me then to my executors. On reflection I have concluded to revoke the contingent bequest of said household furniture to Kate W. Riddle, and it is my will that if neither May S. Kennedy nor Mary C. Speer shall survive me the bequest shall pass immediately to my executors and not to Kate W. Riddie as provided in the foregoing will.

Item Fifth: I hereby revoke the bequest in my foregoing- will of the sum of one thousand (1000.) dollars to the "Woman's Hospital of

Baltimore, Maryland," and I hereby give and bequeath to the St. John's Orphanage of Washington, D.C., the sum of Two thousand (2000.) dollars instead of the sum of One thousand (1000.) dollars bequeathed in my foregoing will.

Item Sixth: I give and bequeath to Robert M. Crawford of the City of Baltimore, Maryland, a life annuity of Five Hundred (500.) dollars, which sum I direct my executors and trustees to pay in equal quarterly installment to said Robert M. Crawford during each and every year of his natural life.

Item Seventh: I hereby change the provisions of the bequest in my foregoing will of five thousand (5000.) dollars for the payment of the expenses of a collegiate course for whichever of the three younger sons of my nephew John N. Lane, brothers of my grand-nephew James Buchanan Lane, will faithfully prepare for the said college course, so as to make the said bequest only to and for the benefit of the youngest but one and the youngest of the sons of my nephew John N. Lane.

Item Eighth: In case I shall not in my lifetime have obtained possession of the portrait hereinafter mentioned I direct my executors to obtain possession as soon as possible after my death of a certain portrait of myself painted by Munzig of New York now in the possession of the artist, the agreed price being fifteen hundred (1500.) dollars, of which agreed price one thousand (1000.) dollars have been paid on account, to the end that the said portrait may be disposed of by my said executors in accordance with a private memorandum addressed to them.

IN TESTIMONY WHEREOF I have hereunto set my hand and seal this 10th day of June 1899

HARRIET LANE JOHNSTON

Signed, sealed, published and declared by the above named testatrix. Harriet Lane Johnston, as and for a codicil to her last will and testament bearing date on June first, 1895, in the presence of us, who, in her presence and to her request and in the presence of each other have subscribed our names as witnesses thereto this 10th day of June, 1899.

JOHN D. JONES
J. VAN NESS PHILIPS
OSCAR LUCKETT

CODICIL

I, Harriet Lane Johnston the above named testatrix hereby make publish and declare this as and for a codicil (No 2) to my foregoing will bearing date on first day of June 1895 and hereto attached.

Item 1st — To William Mann Irvine—President of Mercersburg Academy—Franklin Co. Pennsylvania the sum of $500. to be used by him in having a portrait of President Buchanan painted by a first class artist and to be placed—as he has requested—in the new Dining Hall of that Institution. If this should be considered by my Executors a successful portrait, I request them to have painted by the same artist, a 3/4 size portrait to replace the now faded one hanging in the White House, Washington, D.C. For this purpose I give and bequeath a sum not exceeding $1500.

Item 2nd — The silver cup and small round tray — marked James Buchanan Johnston. I give and bequeath to Robert Lehr Jr. of Baltimore Maryland.

Item 3rd — I give and bequeath my small high silver bowl — (given in my will to Emily Johnston Hoffman) to Rev. William L. Devries of the Pro-Cathedral — Washington, D.C.

Item 4th — The sum appropriated in my Will for three Scholarships in Johns Hopkins University — Baltimore, Maryland — I desire to change from $60.000 to $90.000.

Item 5th — I give and bequeath my many strings of small pearls to my cousin May Selden Kennedy — also my Lily of the Valley diamond brooche (which in my will is given to Pattie Jenkins Lane) I give to May S Kennedy. On the death of May S. Kennedy these pearls & this brooche I give to my niece Pattie J. Lane of Bellefonte-Pennsylvania.

Item 6th — I give and bequeath to May S. Kennedy my portrait just completed by George Munzig of New York — also any one piece of silver she may select that has not been already disposed of.

Item 7th — Instead of the $2,000 — to my niece Pattie Jenkins Lane given in my Will for her education — which is now finished as far as schools are concerned, I give and bequeath the same sum to her absolutely.

IN TESTIMONY WHEREOF I have hereunto set my hand and seal this 2nd day of June 1900.

Signed HARRIET LANE JOHNSTON

Signed, sealed, published and declared by the above named testatrix Harriet Lane Johnston as and for a codicil to her last Will and testament bearing date on June first 1895, in the presence of us, who, in her presence and at her request and in the presence of each other have subscribed our names as witnesses thereto this 2nd day of June 1900.

(Signed) MATTIE W. JOHNSON

(Signed) RALPH C. JOHNSON

(Signed) ROBERT N. CRAWFORD

I, Harriet Lane Johnston, being of sound and disposing mind, memory and understanding, do make, publish and declare this additional codicil to my will dated June first eighteen hundred and ninety five.

WHEBEAS by my said will I bequeathed to my three nephews, John N. Lane, James B. Lane and E. Eskridge Lane, the sum of twenty thousand (20000.) dollars each.

Now I hereby revoke the said legacies, and in lieu thereof give and bequeath unto the Fidelity Trust Company, of Philadelphia,

Pennsylvania, the sum of sixty thousand (60000.) dollars in and upon following trusts: In trust to invest and keep investing some safe income producing property the whole usable fund and to pay over the income therefrom arising in equal shares, quarter-annually to my said three nephews, John N. Lane, James B. Lane, and E. Eskridge Lane, and to the survivors and survivor of them. But upon the death of any one of said nephews leaving lawful issue him surviving, then my said trustee shall forthwith pay over to such issue, per stirpes and not per capita, the same proportion of the principal of said fund which the said nephew was receiving of the income at the time of his death. And should all three of my said nephews die and none of them leave lawful issue surviving, then the said fund of sixty thousand (60000.) dollars shall thereupon fall into and become a part of the general residue of my estate and follow the disposition of such general residue made by my said will dated June 1st, 1895.

WHEREAS by my said will I bequeath to my Executors the sum of fifteen thousand (15000.) dollars in trust for the benefit of my cousin May S. Kennedy;

Now I hereby revoke said bequest for the benefit of my said cousin May S. Kennedy, and in lieu thereof give to my Executors the sum of sixty thousand (60000.) dollars, in trust to invest the same and pay over the income there from to my said cousin May S. Kennedy during her life. And in further trust, should she in writing so request, to invest not exceeding fifteen thousand (15000.) dollars of said sum of sixty thousand dollars in a residence to be purchased or built for her as she may require, to be held by my said Executors in trust to permit her to use and occupy the same during her life. And after the death of the said May S. Kennedy in trust to hold and apply twenty five thousand (25000.) dollars, part of said sum of sixty thousand (60000.) dollars, or any property in which such sum of twenty five thousand (25000.) dollars may be invested, to such uses as my said cousin May S. Kennedy may by last will and testament direct and the balance of thirty five thousand (35000.) dollars to pay over to and distribute among the lawful issue of said May S. Kennedy, if any, per stirpes and per capita. And should my said cousin May S. Kennedy die without leaving lawful issue her surviving, or without having any last will and testament, then and in each such case the portions of said fund of sixty thousand (60000.) dollars hereby directed to be distributed in accordance with her last will and among such lawful issue, respectively, shall become a part of the general residue of my estate and follow the disposition of such general residue made by my said will dated June 1st, 1895.

Whereas by my said will I bequeath to Emily J. Hoffman my ring of six diamonds which was given me by my sister-in-law Margaret P. Johnston; Now I hereby revoke said bequest to said Emily J. Hoffman, and in lieu thereof I give and bequeath to my sister-in-law Margaret P. Johnston the said ring of six diamonds.

I give and bequeath to the Trustees of the Corcoran Gallery of Art, and their successors, the following articles, to wit: (1) a portrait of Lady Essex as Juliet, by Sir Thomas Lawrence, P.R.A.; (2) a portrait of Mrs. Hammond by Sir Joshua Reynolds, P.R.A.; (3) the picture or painting The Valley Farm by John Constable, R.A.; (4) the portrait of Miss Kirkpatrick, 1734-1802, by George Romney, R.A. This portrait was purchased of Messrs. Lowrie and Co., 15 Old Bond Street, who bought it from one of the family for whom it was painted; (5) the portrait of Miss Murray by Sir William Beechy, R.A., 1750-1839; (6) the portrait of "Josepha Boegart," lady in waiting to Marie de Medici, wife of Henry Fourth of France, by Frans Bourbus (the younger); (7) the portrait of "Madame Tulp," perhaps the wife of the famous Dr. Tulp of Rembrandt Celebrity, by Jansen; (8) the portrait of Miss Abington by John Hoppner, R.A., 1758-1810 (9) the painting Madonna and Child by Bernandini Laini, 1460-1530; (10) the painting of Madonna and Child by Berreggio; (11) the portrait of King Edward VII, by Sir John Watson Gordon, painted for President Buchanan and sent to him after the King's visit, (as Prince of Wales) to President Buchanan; also the framed letter of presentation from the Prince; (12) the painting of the President with the Prince of Wales and his suite, the cabinet, etc., at Mt. Vernon, by Rossiter—standing by Washington's Tomb uncovered, whilst the Marine Band played a dirge; (13) the painting A street in India or Cairo by Wickes; (14) the painting Independence by Mayer; (15) the portrait of President Buchanan, when he was about forty years of age, painted just before he went as Minister to Russia, by Eichholtz of Lancaster, Pennsylvania; (16) the portrait of James Buchanan Johnston painted when about fourteen years of age by Harper Pennington; (17) the marble bust of President Buchanan by Dexter of Boston; (18) the marble bust of Mr. Henry E. Johnston by Rhinehart; (19) the marble likeness of my son Henry E. Johnston, when two years old, as Cupid stringing his bow, by Rhinehart; (20) a fine Roman Mosaic, framed; (21) the first message sent over the Atlantic Cable from Queen Victoria and answer by President Buchanan, framed; (22) a very old engraving, framed, of a portrait of John Hampden, presented to President Buchanan by Mr. MacGregor M.P. for Glasgow; (23) the miniature of President Buchanan by Henry Brown of Philadelphia; (24) the photograph, framed, of Queen Victoria, presented to me by her Majesty in June, 1898; (25) large engravings of the Queen and Prince Consort, framed, presented to me by the Prince of Wales through Lord Lyons, when about to leave this country; (26) the silver medal of Princess Royal of England, struck off on her marriage to the Crown Prince of Germany, sent by the Prince Consort to President Buchanan, together with the letter accompanying said medal; (27) letters between her Majesty and President Buchanan on the occasion of the visit of the Prince of Wales to the United States; (28) the bible on which President Buchanan took the oath of office March 4th 1857; and (29) the gaval used at Cincinnati when President Buchanan was nominated June, 1856. Also any additional paintings or other works or art which may be hereafter acquired by me. The medal and the miniature of President Buchanan mentioned above should be placed in a small glass case with the other things of historical value. Provided that the articles hereby bequeathed to The Trustees of the Corcoran Gallery of Art and their successors, shall be kept together in a room, provided for the purpose, in the Corcoran Gallery of Art, and to be designated as "The Harriet Lane Johnston Collection," the place of deposit to be selected and approved by Mr. Ralph C. Johnson and Mr. Blakeslee of New York; and provided further that in the event that the Government, of the United States shall establish in the City of Washington a National Art Gallery, that the said articles shall, upon the establishment of said National Art Gallery, be, by the said Trustees of the Corcoran Gallery of Art and their successors, delivered to the said National Art Gallery, and upon such delivery shall become the absolute property of the said National Art Gallery established by the United States. Should this bequest be not accepted by the Trustees of the Corcoran Gallery of Art under the terms above stated, or for any reason fail, then such of said articles as are, by my will dated June 1st, 1895, specifically disposed of, shall follow the disposition made in my said will of June 1st, 1895, and those not otherwise disposed of are to be sold at private sale by my Executors, which sale shall be conducted under the supervision of Mr. Blakeslee of New York and the proceeds thereof shall become a part of the general residue of my estate and follow the disposition of such general residue made in my said will of June 1st, 1895.

I give and bequeath the marble bust of myself by Rhinehart and the miniature of myself by Henry Brown to my cousin May S. Kennedy for life, and upon her death to Mary C. Speer, for life, and thereafter the said marble bust and the said miniature shall become a part of the foregoing collection of works of art hereinbefore bequeathed to the Trustees of the Corcoran Gallery of Art and follow the disposition of that bequest.

WHEREAS by my said will dated June 1st, 1895, I have given to the Vestry of St. Paul's Episcopal Church of Baltimore, Maryland, my pair of silver candelabra upon certain conditions and in the event of their not being accepted by said Vestry on said conditions I have given the one of said candelabra to Mary C. Speer for life, and then to Patty Jenkins Lane;

Now I hereby modify said bequest so that in the event of the said Vestry not accepting said candelabra on the conditions named the one given to said Mary C. Speer shall go to said Mary C. Speer for life and after her death to my cousin May S. Kennedy for her life, and after her death to the said Patty Jenkins Lane now Mrs. Fay of Altoona, Pennsylvania.

I give and bequeath to the House of Mercy, the institution located at No. 2408 K Street, Northwest, in the City of Washington, District of Columbia, the sum of four thousand (4000.) dollars.

WHEREAS by my said will I appoint my brother-in-law Josiah Lee Johnston and William A. Fisher of the City of Baltimore, State of Maryland, and Calderon Carlisle of the City of Washington, District of Columbia, to be the Executors of my said last will and testament; and whereas said William A. Fisher and said Calderon Carlisle have since died;

Now I hereby nominate, constitute and appoint the said Josiah Lee Johnston of Baltimore, Maryland, D.K. Este Fisher, son of William A. Fisher, of Baltimore, Maryland, William G. Johnson, of the City of Washington, District of Columbia, partner of the late Calderon Carlisle, and my cousin May S. Kennedy, to be the Executors and Executrix of my last will and testament and codicils thereto: and further, should all of the persons named by me as executors die before me, or before completing the administration of my estate, or renounce the officer of executor, then, and in any of said events, I nominate, constitute and appoint the Union Trust and Storage Company of the District of Columbia to be the Executor of my said last will and testament and codicils thereto.

IN WITNESS WHEREOF I have hereunto set my hand and affixed my seal this 21st day of April 1902.

HARRIET LANE JOHNSTON. (Seal.)

Signed, sealed, published and declared by the above named testatrix, Harriet Lane Johnston, as and for an additional codicil to her last will and testament bearing date June 1st, 1895, in our presence, who, at her request, in her presence and in the presence of each other have subscribed our names as witnesses thereto.

RALPH C. JOHNSON
1735 I St N. W.
WILLIAM THOMPSON HARRIS,
1733 I St. N. W.
OSCAR LUCKETT
626 A St. S. E.

I, Harriet Lane Johnston, formerly of the City of Baltimore, in the State of Maryland, but now, and for sixteen years past, domiciled in the City of Washington, in the District of Columbia, which latter place I hereby declare to be my legal domicile, being of sound and disposing mind, do make, publish and declare this codicil to my will dated June first, 1895.

WHEREAS by my said will I give and bequeath to John N. Lane. James Buchanan Lane and Elliott Eskridge Lane all my gold pens and pencils, all the old-time jewelry, which belonged to my mother, all the silverware and set of pink china without the laurel border and the set of white and gilt china which I got from my father, mother and sister and from my uncle James Buchanan, my mother's Embroidery pictures, the small likenesses of my father and my uncle Thomas Lane, the three photographs of my uncle James Buchanan, the chair, walking sticks and canes of my uncle James Buchanan the mahogany furniture from Wheatland and the eleven pictures of the Royal Family given to me by the Prince of Wales:

Now I hereby revoke the said bequest and give and bequeath all of the said articles to my executors in and upon the following trusts, that is to say. In trust to divide all the said articles as nearly as they can be divided into three equal parcels and to assign, transfer and deliver one of said Equal parcels to Patty Jenkins Lane, now Mrs. Fay of Altoona, Pennsylvania, the daughter of the said John N. Lane, and upon such delivery the same shall become her absolute property: to assign transfer and deliver one of said equal parcels to Richard Stockton Lane, son of the said James Buchanan Lane, and upon such delivery the same shall become the absolute property of the said Richard Stockton Lane; to assign transfer and deliver one of said Equal parcels to the said Elliott Eskridge Lane, and upon such delivery the same shall become his absolute property.

WHEREAS, by my said will, I bequeath to Ettie W. Speer Painter, described in my said will as Ettie W. Speer, my diamond heart; Now I hereby revoke the said bequest and bequeath said diamond heart to Mary E. Painter, the daughter of said Ettie W. Speer Painter.

WHEREAS, by my said will, I bequeath my sapphire and diamond ring and the miniature of myself by Brown to my cousin Mary S. Kennedy for her life and after her death to my niece Patty Jenkins Lane; Now I hereby modify said bequests and revoke the provision for my niece Patty Jenkins Lane and bequeath the said sapphire and diamond ring and the said miniature to my said Cousin May S. Kennedy,

WHEREAS, by my said will, I have bequeathed certain articles of jewelry to Mary G. Shapter, of 7 Clarendon Place, Hyde Park Garden, London, England; Now I hereby modify said bequest by revoking the bequest to her of the diamond crescent in said bequest contained.

WHEREAS, by my said will, I have bequeathed to my servant, Eliza Butler, if in my employ at the time of my death or if she should remain in my employ until disabled from work, the sum of five hundred dollars; Now I hereby modify said bequest by increasing the said legacy to the sum of fifteen hundred dollars ($1500.)

WHEREAS, by my said will, I have bequeathed to Patty Jenkins Lane, now Mrs. Fay of Altoona, Pennsylvania the sum of two thousand dollars ($2000.); Now I hereby modify said bequest by increasing the said legacy to her to the sum of five thousand dollars ($5000.)

WHEREAS, by my said will, I bequeathed to the vestry of St. Paul's Episcopal Church, Baltimore, a pair of Silver Candelabra upon certain terms therein set forth and by a codicil dated April 21st 1902 I have modified said bequest as in said Codicil set forth; and whereas, I have since ascertained that said Candelabra are not suitable in design for said St. Paul's Church; Now therefore I hereby revoke said bequest in said will and in said Codicil as to said pair of Candelabra and I give and bequeath to Josiah Lee Johnston the one of said Candelabra which came from his mother's Estate and the other one to Mary C. Speer for her life and after her death to May S. Kennedy, absolutely.

WHEREAS, by the third item of a codicil to my said will, the said codicil being dated June tenth, 1899, I give and devise the farm in Virginia owned by me to my Cousin May S. Kennedy for her life with remainder to her lawful child or children who may be living at her death and in default of such child or children direct the same to become a part of the residue of my estate; Now I hereby modify said devise and give and devise the said farm, in the event of the said May S. Kennedy dying without lawful issue to her sister Mrs. Julia Kennedy Taylor, in fee simple.

WHEREAS, by a codicil to my said will, the said codicil being dated June tenth, 1899, I have bequeathed to the Protestant Episcopal Cathedral Foundation the sum of two hundred thousand dollars ($200.000.), upon certain trusts in said Codicil set forth; Now I hereby modify said bequest by increasing the same to the sum of three hundred thousand dollars ($300.000.) and by these further provisions, namely: That not more than one half of the said sum. That is not exceeding one hundred and fifty thousand dollars ($150.000) shall be used for the construction of the building, which is to be known as the "Lane Johnston Building" the site for which and the necessary appurtenant grounds for which are to be provided by the said Protestant Episcopal Cathedral Foundation, and the balance of said sum of three hundred thousand dollars ($300.000.) not used for the construction of said building shall be invested by said Protestant Episcopal Cathedral Foundation as an endowment fund to be known as the "Lane Johnston Fund" and the income to be used for the maintenance of said school for boys.

While not restricting the general objects of said School it is my wish that the said school shall be so conducted and the said Fund so applied as specially to provide for the free maintenance, education and training of choir-boys, primarily those in the service of the Cathedral. Reposing special confidence in the discretion in this regard of the Rev.

Philip M. Rhinelander I further direct that he shall have charge and supervision of the selection of the site for and construction of the said School building and of the organization and management of the School, but in the event of his death or inability or declination to act the whole of said matters are committed to the said Protestant Episcopal Cathedral Foundation.

WHEREAS, by a Codicil to my said will, which, said Codicil is dated April twenty-first, 1902 I give and bequeath to the Trustees of the Corcoran Gallery of Art the several works of Art and other articles therein set forth, upon certain conditions, among others that they shall be kept together in a room to be provided for the purpose in the Corcoran Gallery of Art and to be designated as the "Harriet Lane Johnston Collection"; Now I hereby modify said bequest and make the same upon this condition, in addition to the other terms and conditions therein contained, which I hereby re-affirm, namely: That the said Trustees of the Corcoran Gallery of Art shall build an annex to the Art Gallery, to be approved by the said Mr. Blakeslee, or should he not be living or should he decline to act, then to be approved by my executors, which said annex shall not be provided with any means for artificial heat and shall be so constructed and arranged as to protect, as far as possible from the heat of Summer the articles therein deposited. My reason for this condition is that many of the said pictures bequeathed to the said Trustees of the Corcoran Gallery of Art are of a character to become cracked and ultimately ruined if deposited in a place subject to the heat ordinarily maintained in said Art Gallery, and are such as require, for their preservation, to be kept in a depository of low temperature; and it is my belief that, if a suitable annex, as above described be provided, the said Trustees will be the recipients of other gifts of valuable paintings which the owners would be unwilling to have deposited in the present Gallery subject to the thermal conditions there existing.

WHEREAS, by said Codicil dated April twenty-first, 1902. I have bequeathed to my executors the sum of Sixty thousand dollars ($60,000) in and upon certain trusts for the benefit of my Cousin May S. Kennedy; Now I hereby revoke said bequest and in lieu thereof I give and bequeath to my said cousin, May S. Kennedy, absolutely, the sum of one hundred thousand dollars ($100,000.) I also give and bequeath to my said Cousin May S. Kennedy my Silver tea-set of seven pieces which was given to me and my husband by my brother-in-law, Josiah Lee Johnston, and also such one of my silver/tea-trays as my said Cousin, May S. Kennedy may select; and I also give to my said cousin, May S. Kennedy, the entire furniture of my bed-room hereby revoking anything in my said will or any codicil thereto inconsistent with this bequest to her of the said bed-room furniture.

I give and bequeath to my said Cousin, May S. Kennedy, the set of India China in daily use by me.

WHEREAS, by my said will, I have given to Mary C. Speer five thousand dollars ($5,000); now I hereby modify said bequest by increasing the said legacy to her to the sum of ten thousand dollars ($10,000).

WHEREAS, by my said will, I have given to Kate W. Riddle the sum of one thousand dollars ($1000.), Now I hereby modify said bequest by increasing the said legacy to her to the sum of three thousand dollars ($3000).

I give and bequeath to Louise Speer the sum of three thousand dollars ($3000.)

To Letitia Bobler, colored, should she survive me, I give and bequeath the sum of two hundred dollars ($200.).

I give and bequeath to the National Homeopathic Hospital, now located at the corner of Second and N Streets, Northwest, in the City of Washington the sum of one thousand dollars ($1000.).

I give and bequeath to my Executors the sum of two thousand dollars ($2000) in trust to pay over the same to the Rev. Philip M. Rhinelander, or to whomsover may at the time be Rector of the Episcopal Church known as the Chapel of the Good Shepherd on Sixth Street between H and I Streets, Northeast, in the City of Washington for the benefit of the Construction of the new church.

WHEREAS, by the will of my late husband, Henry E. Johnston, power and authority are vested in me to dispose by my last will and testament of the entire residuum of his Estate; and, whereas, by my will dated June first, 1895 and the several codicils thereto I have intended to exercise the power of disposition, over said entire residue of my late husband's estate; Now, to obviate any question as to the purpose of my said will and said codicils and the true interpretation thereof, I hereby give, bequeath and devise unto my Executors, in addition to all my individual property, the entire rest and residue of the estate real and personal of my late husband, Henry E. Johnston, given, devised and bequeathed by his said will to Josiah Lee Johnston, William A. Fisher and W. Graham Bowdoin, their survivors or survivor, and their heirs, personal representatives, successors and assigns, subject to disposition by me; and I hereby appoint my Executors to receive the said Entire rest and residue of the Estate of my said deceased husband, but in trust nevertheless to apply the same, together with all other property over which I have the power of disposition by will, in the manner and for the uses and purposes declared and set forth in my said last will and the several codicils thereto including this Codicil.

IN TESTIMONY WHEREOF I have hereunto set my hand and affixed my seal this eighteenth day of March, A.D. 1903.

HARRIET LANE JOHNSTON (Seal)

Signed, Sealed, published and declared by the above named testatrix, Harriet Lane Johnston and for a codicil to her last will and testament bearing date on June first, 1895, in our presence who in her presence, at her request and in the presence of each other have subscribed our names as witnesses thereto.

WALDEN MYER.

SARAH D. SPEER.

CHAS. E. SPEER

I, Harriet Lane Johnston, of the City of Washington, in the District of Columbia, but now temporarily sojourning at Narragansett Pier, Rhode Island, do make and publish the following as and for an additional Codicil to my Last Will and Testament, that is to say:

I Give and Bequeath to Mrs. Julia O. Kennedy the sum of Three Thousand Dollars ($3,000.)

IN TESTIMONY WHEREOF I have hereunto set my hand and Seal this second day of July, 1903.

HARRIET LANE JOHNSTON (Seal)

Signed, Sealed, Published and Declared by Harriet Lane Johnston, the above named Testatrix, as and for a Codicil to her Last Will and Testament, in the presence of us, who, at her request, in her presence, and in the presence of each other, have hereunto subscribed our names as the witnesses thereto.

MYRA L. DRAKE,

1110 L Street N.W.

Washington D.C.

HENRY KROGSTAD

1524 K St. Washington D.C

Annex C
James Buchanan's Will

Last Will and Testament of James Buchanan[116]

IN THE NAME OF GOD, AMEN!

I James Buchanan, late President of the United States, in the humble hope of Salvation through the merits and atonement of my Lord and Saviour, Jesus Christ, do make and publish the following as my last will and testament.

1. I direct that my body shall be interred in the Woodward Cemetery, in a plain and simple manner and without parade.

2. I direct that my debts, (which are small) and my funeral expenses shall be paid by my Executors out of my personal estate not herein specifically bequeathed.

3. I give and bequeath to my niece Harriet Lane Johnston, wife of Henry E. Johnston, my brother Rev. Edward Y. Buchanan, and my nephew J. Buchanan Henry, all the books, plate, beds and bedding and all the house hold and kitchen furniture belonging to me and in my dwelling house at Wheatland at the time of my decease, to be equally divided between by themselves; they allowing Esther Parker two hundred dollars worth of the same free of charge; and it is my will that no inventory or appraisement be made of these articles.

4. I give and bequeath to my brother Edward Y. Buchanan, all my wearing apparel, my gold watch, watch chain, and seals.

5. I give and bequeath to my valued friend, Esther Parker, who has long been a faithful and useful member of my family the sum of Five Thousand Dollars, which with Two Thousand Dollars already given to her she well deserved, and I commend her to the kindness of all my relatives after my decease.

6. I give and bequeath to the City of Lancaster, my two certificates of Loan Nos. 42 & 43 from us that said City, for One Thousand Dollars each, or in case I shall dispose of them in my life time, then the sum of Two Thousand Dollars instead thereof in trust to employ the annual interest of the same in purchasing fuel for the use of the poor and indigent females of the City of Lancaster, during the winter season. This bequest is to be incorporated with the fund of Four Thousand Dollars provided by me some years ago for the same purpose and is to be administered in the same manner by the City Authorities.

7. I give and bequeath to the Presbyterian Church of the City of Lancaster, of which I am a member of the sum of One Thousand Dollars.

8. I direct that all the real estate of which I may die seized shall be sold by my Executors, either at public or private sale, when in their opinion this will best promote the interest of my residuary Legatees and conveyed by them or the survivor of them to the purchaser or purchasers in fee simple.

9. It is my will that the proceeds of the sales of my real estate with the rents issues and profits whereof together with the whole of my remaining personal estate, of whatever nature or kind, this may be, shall be divided and distributed among my relatives, and the following proportions, to wit: I give and bequeath the one fourth part of the same to my niece Harriet Lane Johnston, the daughter of my deceased sister, Jane B. Lane; and I give and bequeath another fourth part thereof to my brother Edward Y. Buchanan, and it is my will that neither of these shall be charged with the considerable advancements I have made to each of my lifetime. I give and bequeath the one fifth part of the same to my nephew J. Buchanan Henry, the surviving child of my deceased sister, Harriet B. Henry. It is my will that the remaining portion of this my estate shall be divided into three equal parts, the first part thereof, I give and bequeath to John N. Lane, James B. Lane, Elliott E. Lane, minor sons of my deceased nephew, James B. Lane, and to the survivors or survivor of them; — another equal third part thereof; I give and bequeath to my niece Mary E. Dunham, the daughter of my deceased sister, Maria T. Yates; and the remaining third part thereof, I give and bequeath to Maria B. Weaver, Jessie Magaw, formerly Jessie Weaver, James B. Weaver and John Bless Weaver, minor children of my deceased niece Jessie Magaw Weaver and the grand children of my deceased sister, Maria, by her first husband Dr. Jesse Magaw, and to the survivors or survivor of them.

And it is my will that my executors shall retain in their own hands the amount of the legacy of the three minor sons of James B. Lane, with its accumulations, and as each of them shall severally attain the age of twenty-one, pay over to him the share to which he may then be entitled, and it is also my will that my executors shall retain in their hands the amount of the Legacy to the four minor children of my niece Jessie Magaw Weaver, with its accumulations and as each of them shall severally attain the age of twenty-one pay over to him or her the share to which he or she may be then entitled. Should my Executors deem it necessary for the maintenance and education of the two younger of these children to wit: — James B. Weaver and John Bless Weaver, they may apply the interest and even a portion of the principal of their respective shares for this purpose but under their own immediate directions.

Whilst feeling full confidence both in the integrity and eminent business capacity of Edward E. Johnston, the husband of my niece, Harriet Lane Johnston, I yet deem it prudent to secure to her a maintenance against the unforeseen contingencies of future years. For this purpose I appoint my hereinafter named Executors Hiram B. Swarr and Edward Y. Buchanan, or the survivor of them, trustees or trustee, and direct them to retain in their hands, and invest and manage to the best advantage free and discharged from the debts and control of her said husband, the two thirds of the amount bequeathed to her as one of my residuary legatees under this my will, in trust that they or the survivor of them, shall pay to her annually or semi-annually the interest accruing thereupon for her sole and separate use during the life of her said husband, and her separate receipts for the same shall be sufficient acquittance.

And on these further trusts, that should the Harriet Lane Johnston survivor her said husband, then to pay to her the principal of the fund thus created. Should she die and his lifetime, have at having a child or children, then in trust to pay to such child or children or the survivor or survivors of them, or their lawfully appointed Guardians for their use and their property, the whole of the said fund. But should the said Harriet Lane Johnston, die in the lifetime of her said husband, without leaving a child or children then it is my will that this will that the said Trustees or the survivor of them shall pay the whole of this said fund to the children of my brother Edward Y. Buchanan, and to my nephew J. Buchanan Henry, and to the survivors or survivor of them all, share and share alike to whom I give and bequeath the same.

And finally I apply my brother Edward Y. Buchanan and my trusty friend Hiram B. Swarr, to be the Executors and Executor of this my last Will and Testament.

Give under my hand and seal, at Wheatland in the County of Lancaster this twenty-seventh day of January, one thousand eight hundred and sixty-six.

James Buchanan

Declared and published by the testator to be his Last Will and Testament in the presence of us.

W. W. Brown

J. W. F. Swift

I, James Buchanan, do hereby add this codicil to my last will and testament dated on the 27th January 1866, Viz.: —

I direct that my executors shall apply towards the payment of the residuary Legacy left to my nephew, J. Buchanan Henry, by my last will and testament, the principal and interest due upon the bond from him to me, dated on the 15th June, 1866, for some of Fourteen thousand and fifty dollars ($14,650.00)

ITEM:- I give and bequeath to Martha J. Lane, the widow of my deceased nephew James B. Lane, a legacy of Two Thousand Dollars.

Given under my hand and seal at Wheatland this twenty-ninth day of April one thousand eight hundred and sixty-seven

JAMES BUCHANAN

This is a codicil to be added to and taken as a part of the last will and testament of me James Buchanan.

I hereby direct my Executors named in my last will and testament to place all the papers, correspondence and private and public documents connected with my public life in the hands of my friend, William B. Reed, who having shown to me in my retirement great kindness and in whom I have entire confidence to enable him to prepare such a biographical work I desire. With this view I direct my Executors to pay to the order of William B. Reed, such sums in the aggregate not exceeding one thousand dollars, as may be necessary in his opinion to secure the proper publication of such biographical work, and in case it or any part of it is not so used it shall go into the remainder of my estate.

As some compensation for the work which Mr. Reed has undertaken to perform I give and bequeath to his wife, Mrs. Mary L. Reed, sum of Five Thousand Dollars which I direct to be a legacy for her separate use and benefit, and in case of her death for her children, said amount to be paid to her on the completion of the work, or in the event of her death, before that then to her children.

I give and bequeath to Peter Hillyer, Mary Smithgall and Lizer Stoner, domestics now with me, or lately in my employ, each the sum of one hundred dollars.

In witness whereof I have hereunto set my hand and seal at Wheatland this twenty-ninth day of August, A.D. one thousand eight hundred and sixty-seven (1867)

JAMES BUCHANAN (Seal)

Signed, sealed and declared by the said James Buchanan, as and for a codicil to his last will and in the presence of us.

J. B. Baker

Eliza Guest.

I declare the following to be codicil TO MY LAST WILL AND TESTAMENT, dated the 27th day of January, 1867.

I give and devise unto Harriet Lane Johnston, the wife of Henry E. Johnston, and to her heirs and assigns my dwelling house at Wheatland, and tract of land connected therewith, containing about twenty-two acres with the appurtenances; and I charge her for the same the sum of Twelve Thousand Dollars. In the settlement of my estate she is to account to my Executors for this sum of money and it is to be deducted from the residuary share of my estate bequeathed to her under my will.

Given under my hand and seal at Wheatland, in the County of Lancaster this thirty-first day of August, one thousand eight hundred and sixty-seven.

JAMES BUCHANAN

Annex D
Complete Texts of Referenced Correspondence

Selma, Alabama[117]
June 20, 1839
Dear Buchanan,

Returning to my home after an absence of several weeks your friendly & most acceptable letter was handed to me. I can but feel gratified at the lively interest you attach to me in what you suppose I have so much at hand, but I assure you my Friend it is a matter in which I have not taken the interest you imagine & I shall without any feeling of subject give my cordial support to any Republican who may be designated by a Convention is in any other way presented as the Candidate of the party. I have not moved a finger in anyone's behalf, but have considerably avoided any demonstrations of problems said that which by committing my Friendly support when the nomination is much disappointing & ratify them, & this operates unfavorably upon the Presidential election.

...

If Pres. Martin Van Buren I've said act with his usual prudency & may do himself & the party much mischief with me & my Friends for respect our feelings & not so interested as to make it a matter of serious importance, but I know that the Bander & Thandall party & not warmly engaged in the cause of Colonel Polk, & should succeed in the canvass for Gov. of Tennessee, he will be pressed with all their thought & influence upon the Convention & if defeated by the interference of the President, he will find lukewarm friends in those who move about in professions of devoted attachment the sooner the question is put to rest than better let the individual selected be whom he may.

...

Can it be possible that our little President will support himself to be used by these men?

...

I shall set out for the mountains in a few days, to ramble I know not where, perhaps to the Virginia Springs, but this will entirely depend upon the wish of a jester whose wretched health is my principle inducement for traveling. Nicholas is in good health & spirits.

Your Friend Sincerely
William R. King

HL

Washington 16 February 1842[118]

My dear Harriet

Your letter afforded me very good pleasure. There is no wish nearer my heart that you should become an amiable & intelligent woman; and I am rejoiced to learn that you shall continue at the head of your class. You can render yourself very dear to me by your conduct; and I anticipate with pleasure the months which I trust in heaven we may pass together after the adjournment of Congress. I expect to be in Lancaster for a week or ten days about the first of April when I hope to see you in good health & receive the most favorable reports of your behavior.

Rick Yates Henry is now a midshipman in the Navy. He is now at Boston on board the John Adams & will sail in a few days for the Brasilian station. He will probably be aboard for two or three years. He is much pleased with the situation. I trust that his conduct may do both himself & his friends honor. When he left they were all well except your Aunt Maria who complains of a cough. Elizabeth is better than she has been for years.

I send you $13, — the remains of poor Buck's among when he arrived here. It was of no use to him & would be of no use to me here. Please hand it to your brother James & tell him to place it to my credit for what it is worth.

When you write to your sister Mary, give her my kindest & best love.

Remember me affectionately to your brother James, Miss Hetty, the Miss Crawfords and believe me to be ever your affectionate uncle. May Heaven bless you!

James Buchanan

HL

Paris, July 1, 1844[119]

My Dear Friend [James Buchanan]

I sailed for New York as you are aware on the 10th May. The voyage was not a very long one being only 22 days, but surprisingly unpleasant as both Mrs. Ellis & myself were seasick with but little intermission until we arrived at France; we were consequently much exhausted from want of food & drink & have not even yet fully recovered from its effects. I was met by the Americans here with great cordiality who seemed to be much delighted that our country was after so long an interval again represented by a full Minister — I found our Friend Roosevelt at the Rail Road Depot to remain since having delayed his departure for some days to shake me by my hand. I saw Mrs. Roosevelt the next morning & handed her your letter. She is in fine health; in fact I never saw her looking better; she expressed great pleasure in hearing from you. They set out the next day for England, intending to return to the United States this summer. Mrs. Roosevelt would have gladly spent the next winter in this gay city; & for myself I shall have been truly gratified to have enjoyed her agreeable society; but her Lord had made up his mind for London, & like a good wife, she submitted with good grace. Immediately upon my arrival, I set about making the necessary arrangements, preparations to my presentation to the King, but so slow were my movements of those important Gentlemen the Sailors that more than two weeks elapsed before I could procure the appropriate uniform.

I then saw Mr. Guigot, the Minister of Foreign Affairs, who promised to take the orders of his Majesty, & today I make my bow to the King. ... I had prepared a short address to his Majesty & I am really ashamed to say that in attempting to deliver it, I became not a little embarrassed & as my nervous system is a good deal shattered by the continued sickness of the voyage, my hands trembled like an alarmed school boy before the dreaded Pedagogue — so much for my Democratic independence. I was mortified & provoked myself on finding that I possessed so evasive a spirit. I managed however to get through after a fashion & received a most flattering answer abounding in warm professions of friendship & respect for the people & government of the United States. My unfortunate delivery convinces me that I am not fitted for diplomacy, & caused me to regret still more that I ever considered to accept of a situation for which I am so illy qualified. All this is for yourself alone, from whom I disguise nothing; but it had determined me absolutely to avail myself of the earliest occasion which offers to get back to my own country & persist our high spirited & proud people to be represented here by some one who has more of the spirit of a man.

I was greatly surprised at the nomination of Polk. He is a very inferior man; and unless the Texas question generally aids him, has no earthly chance of being elected. I hardly know whether it is desirable that he should so far as respects the permanent interests of the Democratic Party; still was I at home, he should have my support. Any man, but Clay.

I was prepared for the ratification of the Texas treaty, but not for Col. Berit & Bill. Is not his concern a strange one; & will it not destroy him with our party?; personal hostility for Tyler & Calhoun alone seems to less guarantee his course. Texas must not be obtained through their agency; & acting upon those motives, he has in all probability lost it to us forever. It is such to be found that this government is strongly inclined to act in concert with England on the subject of Texas. I shall see Mr. Guigot tomorrow or the next day & will if practicable warm to his views. But the thing what they may, they should have not the slightest influence upon our action on the subject. Texas once annexed, & all difficulties are attained England will complain loudly of our grasping spirit & will want of good faith towards Mexico that will be all; She will even be cautious not to put herself in a position of which she can be suspected of encouraging Mexico to make a hostile demonstration. She cannot with safety risk a war with us & without her. Mexico dare not move a finger the course of France would be even more pacific, for there can be no question that this government sees that its commercial interests would be protected by accusations & it cares not a pinch of salt whether slavery exists in Texas or not. But, the treaty has unfortunately been rejected & in this state of things you must not be prepared to find England preparing France ... to guaranty the independence of Texas without conditions; & force Mexico to acknowledge it. To this France will in all probability accept, as Louis Phillip is very anxious to cultivate the most friendly relations with England, as is, his Prime Minister Guigot & particularly as we having referred to me the country, such a course will not involve serious difficulties with us. In every respect the rejection of the Treaty was most unfortunate & well as I have already stated probably lose us that friendly country forever. The desire to make Mr. Clay President as part of the Whigs & Mr. Van Buren as that of certain leading Democrats has subjected our country to this misfortune. They have never twist & turn & make excuses, but if our people feel as I do, their political days will be numbered.

July 3. Last night I saw Mr. Guigot at his reception & he was appreciably very cordial, but the numbers of persons present prevented me from having an informal conversation with him relative to Texas, & I had intended [to seek] an early occasion to bring that subject to his notice.

July 5. With yesterday being the 4 of July, I dined with the King of the French. The American Legation was the only persons of the corps Diplomatic invitees, this skews the King's tact if not his friendliness for our Country. Many members of the Royal Family, now in Paris, with the exception of the Duchess of Orleans, was present. I was placed on the left of the Queen. ... The dinner was excellent & the Queen most gracious conversing with me in the most easy & familiar manner during the whole period we remained at the table. In returning to the salon, I had a conversation of fully a half hour with the King, who took occasion to introduce the subject of the Texas Treaty by inquiring what were the reasons which has coursed the rejection by the Senate. This furnished me the opportunity I so much desired & I not only answered his question by stating that the reasons which influenced Senators are various but principally growing out of the pending Presidential Election. But that I wished his majority distinctly to understand that the rejection of the treaty under the peculiar circumstances would not prevent the [present] government from persevering in its efforts to procure the annexation of Texas. That I had every reason to believe that a large majority of the American People would be found in favor of the measure & that their will could not be resisted lest who would be elected President. That any attempt by any present government to obtain a control direct or indirect over that country would not fear to meet with prompt resistance. That we did not anticipate any such attempt except on which part of England with whom we had many points of collision while with France we had none that England was jealous of our growth as a nation & would not hesitate to resort to any measures calculated to retard it & impair our prosperity; but that the interests of France & of the United States were promoted by the same course & I felt convinced that his Majesty's Government would never be found acting in concert with England in this matter.

The King made a strong profession of friendship for the United States; admitted that England had motives for interference which did not & could not apply to France which had no possessions on the American continent that France desired to remain on amicable relations both with England & America. That his government having acknowledged the independence of Texas & entered into a commercial treaty with her, he would prefer seeing her independence secured & the commercial aspects get secured to France by the Treaty uninterrupted but from the whole lesson of his conversation he left my mind strongly unchanged with the connection or that enunciations to the United States would produce no actions on his part of an unfriendly character. How far we may rely upon these assurances time must determine as every motion will be made by England to induce France to unite with her in her efforts to prevent Texas from becoming part of the United States.

Why do I not hear from you? Pack it after Parcel arrived but brings me no letters. This verifying the old adage, out of sight out of mind. ... Mrs. Ellis begins to improve in health & spirits; she says the nomination of Polk has almost made her a Whig. I hope it will not have a similar effect upon many of our heretofore good Democrats. I find it impracticable to procure good Madeira Wine in France & although it is but little used yet I wish to have a special supply for the especial benefit of my Countrymen shall I ask a favor of you to procure for me six dozen of Bringants $15 wine & six of his $12 & course it to be shipped as soon as practicable to have to the care of our consul Mr. Beasly. I will not trouble you with a matter so foreign to your person could I rely upon a Wine Merchant to do me justice? Pay for it, & I will send you a draft as my factor for the account. In this making you both Merchant & Banker. I can only say that I will afford no sincere pleasure to act in the double capacity, whenever you may require any articles they produce of France.

Farewell by Dear Friend & believe me to be as ever devotedly yours.

William R. King

HL

Washington City Feb 17th 1845[120]
Sir [James Buchanan]
The principles and policy which will be observed and maintained during my administration are [stated] in the Resolutions adopted by the Democratic National Committee of Delegates assembled at Baltimore in May last, and in the Inaugural address which I propose to deliver to my Fellow Citizens on assuming the duties of President of the United States and which is herewith handed to you for your perusal. —

In making up my Cabinet, I desire to solicit Gentlemen who agree with me in opinion and who will cordially co-operate with me in carrying out the principles and policy.

In my official action I will myself take no part between gentlemen of the Democratic party who may become aspirants or candidates to succeed me in the Presidential office, and desire that no members of my Cabinet shall do so. — Individual preferences it is not expected or desired to limit or restrain. It is official interference by the disposition of public patronage or otherwise — that I desire to guard against. Should any member of my Cabinet become a candidate for the Presidency or Vice Presidency of the United States, it will be expected upon that happenings of such an event — that he will retire from the Cabinet.

I disapprove the practice which has sometimes [presented] of Cabinet officers absenting themselves for long periods of time from the seat of Government, and having the management of their Departments to Chief clerks or other less responsible persons than themselves. — I expect myself to remain constantly at Washington — unless it may be that no public duty requires my presence — when I may occasional absent, but this only for a short time — that the President and his Cabinet can have any opinion that abuses will be prevented — and that the subordinate Executive offices committed with them respectively will faithfully perform their duty.

If Sir; you concur with me in these opinions and desires, I shall be pleased to have your assistance in my administration as a member of my Cabinet and now tender to you the office of Secretary of State, and invite you to take charge of that Department.

I shall be pleased to view your answer at your earliest convenience.

I am with quiet respect Your able Servant
James K. Polk

HL

Confidential[121]
Paris April 20, 1845
My Dear Friend [James Buchanan]

I had the pleasure to receive by the last steamer your most acceptable letter of the 18 & 19 of March. Great must have been the [drain on you] the swarm of hungry officers seekers have given you and knowing & I do your impatience of spirit when thus beset, I fear you have not in your intercourse with them secured within their favor or future support. You should have received their affectations with kindness and in disappointing their hopes sent them away charmed with your affability. As Col. Polk's back is broad would it not do well to saddle him with the brothers of Gov. Jackson ... Col. Polk might do the same without the slightest inconvenience; [rendered] as I see it insinuated by letter writers he desires a vindication. Is there any foundation for their rumors? There was an article in the Nashville Union which stated most unkindly that you had been appointed to the State Department with an assurance on your part that you would not be a candidate for the Presidency in 1848. Such a statement from that quarter is well calculated to lead to the conclusion that the Col. will not be disposed to relinquish power at the end of four years. — You state that Col. Polk's administration had commenced prosperously and he is determined to know no cliques in parties in the Democratic ranks. I rejoice to know it. It is an evidence of the good sense and sound discretion which I have ever attributed to him; but I will require all his firmness to enable him to preserve in this wise and salutary course. The various sections of the party will put any engine in motion to obtain control in his councils to advance their schemes of personal agrandisement [sic] and fading in this will in all probability become hostile. With whatever appearance of cordiality Calhoun may have left Washington, he feels most deeply his removal from the Sate Department when I know he was very desirous to continue and renders I am greatly deceived you will before one finds his political friends like warm supporters or decided opponents to Col. Polk's administration. I know <u>him</u> and <u>them</u> and as our Friend King said they will rule or ruin. The appointment of many has not given satisfaction to Van Buren & Wright. Flagg was their man and they were much disappointed in not having their wishes complied with so that their support and as far as they can control it that of New York will probably not be cordial. Benton partakes of the same feeling and in addition is not a little scared at finding that his course on the Texas question has impaired his popularity and greatly I understand his prospects for the Presidency.

Naturally of a harsh & overbearing disposition it is to be found that in his present frame of mind he will be but too ready to take office and give trouble. Cass will in all things look to self. So will Woodling. While your colleague Walker will use the immense patronage of the Treasury to advance his relative Dollars. Thus it seems to me there is a beautiful prospect for intrigue and discretion. Now my earnest desire is that you shut your eyes in appearance at least to all those things. Judiciously avoid the manifestations of suspicion. Treat all with marked attention; even with kindness. Participate in none of the squabbles which may take place among them and you will not fail to occupy the vantage ground before the Country. You will I trust pardon me for intruding my advice upon you and attribute it to its true course. I desire to see you placed in the highest office in the government. Col. Polk should not suffer the pressures from office seekers to force him to adopt a course of presumption particularly in the subordinate officers removals in them should only be made because of the importance of the incumbent for a proper discharge of the duties; never upon the political grounds solely. The indiscriminate removals which has of late years pervaded mostly for the purpose of surrounding political friends has done more to degrade and demoralize our people than all other courses put together.

Let me again request that the Consul here (Mr. Walker) may not be removed. I find him succeedingly useful in collecting information and in giving publicity to such articles as I conceive to be important to place before the French public. He is withal an excellent consul. Old Beasley was spared by Gen. Jackson and I hope he will be by Col. Polk. One word as to my friend Washington Irving — He is poor and his position at Madrid is therefore of great importance to him; and his literary imputations give to him a much higher standing then would probably be acquired by a new man. Wheaton's wife his here, she relies on your friendship for her Husband for his succeeding. I have heretofore given you my opinion as to his successfulness. He is decidedly one of the ablest men we have abroad. — The transfer of the Globe to other hands was I have no doubt essential to the harmony of the Democratic Party, but I am not prepared to say to the selection of its future conductors as I designated by you is the best which could have been made to affect that desirable object. Ritchen is indeed a gentleman and although occasionally he runs into error is in them remains correct in his principles. ...

Donaldson's absence from Texas at so important and critical a moment can scarcely be secured. He should have been at his post counteracting by all the means in his power the efforts which the British and French Ministers in conjunction with James, Houston and Smith are making to dissatisfy the People of Texas with the terms of annexation as proposed by Congress. James is an unprincipled Yankey [sic] who obtained his present position by professing to be in favor of annexation and more to retain it is ready to avail himself of any pretext to oppose the measure. To decend [sic] willingly to the rank of private citizen is more than can be expected from the patriotism of such a man. Houston is a visionary and enthusiast; and is coursed away by the seductious idea of planting the Lone Star on the Walls of Montezuma. ...[the] little yankey school master [hopes to] find himself Secretary of State and hopes to be President. He is the author of the articles which have appeared in the Galveston Register. — There can be no question that a vary large proportion of the people of Texas are most anxious to be annexed to the United States, and had the terms proposed been as liberal as they should have been, James & company would not have dared to raise their voices against it. I am however compelled to confess that the terms are illerable [sic] even unjust towards Texas and furnishes to England grounds to operate upon which may provide a change in the public mind unless the President avails himself of the power given him and concedes something more to Texas. This should be done without delay or it may prove too late and that fine country be lost to us forever.

There is scarcely any sacrifice which England would not make to prevent Texas from coming into our possession. France is acting in concert with her, so far as influence goes, but will stop there. She will make no precuniary [sic] sacrifices. I have weighed well the contents of your last dispatch and as you give me full discretion in the matter, I have come to the conclusion that in the present thrust among the state or our relations with England no good purpose could be effected by convicting Mr. Guigot of the prior duplicity of which he had been quietly and especially as it is to be hoped that the question of annexation has before this been differentially settled.

The notice taken of the President's inaugural as the Oregon question in both Houses of Parliament has scared up a war spirit in that country which pervades all classes and caused the detention of the steamer which should have left on the 4th to take out dispatches to Mr. Packinhous. As the excitement was then at its height it was supposed that their instructions contained an ultimatum which was to yield nothing beyond the causing proposition. Should this be the determination of that government negotiations must occur for to such terms we can now accede. I am indeed however to believe for conversations I have held with Mr. Ellis now in Paris who is connected with the Ministry being a Brother in Law of Lord Pipon and himself a Privy Counselor that Mr. Packinhouse's instructions will be of a conciliatory character and that they have great hopes of being able to settle the matter upon fair and liberal terms but of this you are probably much better informed than he is — I am still of the opinion that we should not hesitate to divide the territory (Oregon) by fixing our northern boundary at the latitude of 49. To settle the question I would yield something more and take the southern share of the straits of

Fuceau [sic] and thus give to England the whole of the Van Couvers [sic] Island. Such a variation of the prospectus, which was rejected by Mr. Carning would afford Sir. Robert Pul grounds to stand on and might facilitate an arrangement. I fully understand the difficult position you occupy as regards this question; looking to the generally secured opinion that our title of the whole of the territory is unquestionable. Now after having given to the subject much attention, weighed well the grounds upon which each government rests its claim; I am compelled to come to the conclusion that our title is not perfectly clear and unquestionable; but that a most pleasurable and what might be considered by a many a sound argument might be made against it. If I am correct in this view of the matter, should it not be settled by mutual concessions; and failing to agree upon the extent of those concessions; should it not resort to an arbitration? I throw out these suggestions for your considerations.— I submitted to Doctor Martin your proposition to make him Chief Clerk of the State Department and left it entirely to himself to determine whether he would accept or remain in his present position. He expressed in strong terms his grateful render of your kindness, but having embarked in Diplomacy and having rewards pleased with the situation he occupies would prefer retaining it to a return to the United States at this time. He will write to you himself on the subject. To my native land next autumn; but if circumstances should in the instruction of the President require me to remain at this Court for a longer period I shall certainly do so at whatever inconvenience to myself. The warm weather has improved my health & I propose visiting some watering place in the summer. To try the effect that hot water will have on my rheumatism. Should our difficulties with England be adjusted as I sincerely hope they may be; I shall feel no hesitation in asking for permission to return at present & will not do so because I honestly believe that I have acquired a standing here which would enable me to serve my Country in the event of a war with England more effectually than a new man however superior to me a talent possibly couldn't. I send you several pamphlets on American affairs which have been extensively circulated that you may see how we are opinionating. Also a speech by Dupin in the Chamber of Peers. I wish you to read the marked paragraphs. Present me most kindly to my Friends the Blains and Pleasontons. Also to Mrs. Ogla Taylor and ask her if she intends to make a present of the $100 she placed in my hands; and if not, to inform me what disposition I shall make of it? Mrs. Ellis requests to be kindly remembered to you; and to say that she was a decided advocate of Col. Polk and greatly rejoiced at the defeat of Clay. My best respects to Walker and his excellent Lady. Do not condemn this long letter to the Flames without reading it.
    Your Friend Sincerely,
    William R. King

H L

1847[122]
Philadelphia
Sir — The undersigned, a committee appointed by the friends of JAMES BUCHANAN, in the City and County of Philadelphia, anxious to obtain such information as may be of service in promoting the election of our distinguished fellow citizens to the Presidency of the United States, have been induced to address you, for the purpose of ascertaining the sentiments of our Democratic fellow-citizens in your own county and neighborhood.

As the canvass is now actively progressing, it becomes an important object to spread as much information as can be obtained, before the Democracy of Philadelphia, at as early a date as possible.

In congratulating you on the prospect of the success of 'PENNSYLVANIA'S FAVORITE SON,' we beg of you to favor us with an early answer.

Very respectfully, &c.,

Committee: GEORGE PLITT, DAVID WEBSTER, WILLIAM F. IRELAND, JOHN W. RYAN, PETER RAMBO, WILLIAM LITTLE, JOHN F. BELSTERLING.

Please direct your answer to GEORGE PLITT, Philadelphia.

H L

Wheatland, near Lancaster 13 May 1850[123]
My dear Sir/ [William R. King]
I received your favor of the 8th. Instant, I regret that for the first time, we differ radically before a question which I deem of such vast importance as the Nicaragua Treaty. If it were stripped of all stipulations except those relating immediately to the canal, I would not enter into any Treaty engagement with England even on the single front. The question was well & carefully considered by Mr. Polk's cabinet at the home of the New Granada Treaty & we determined that whilst we would use our good offices, if necessary to provide upon Great Britain to enter unto a similar Treaty to our own with New Grenada, we would not ourselves be a party to any Treaty whatever with G.B. relating to or connected with any territory on part of this North American continent. But this is a very small affair compared with the right which has been assumed by Great Britain & yielded to us to limit us our progress on this continent throughout all future time.

But as you are already committed, I shall say no more on the subject & would not have written to you at all, had I known you had consulted the Democratic Senators upon the Treaty before its signature & obtained their consent to it in advance. This shows the great influence of your opinions, an influence I consider well deserved & immensely beneficial. You have however, in my humble opinion, subjected fire on this occasion.

You ask my opinion on the Compromise reported by the Committee of Thirteen. On this subject you are better qualified to judge than myself. I have always believed that the real difference in practical effect between non intervention & the Wilmot Proviso was that between tweedle dum & tweedle dee. Non intervention however saves the feelings of the South & enables them to triumph over the free soilers. I was convinced in equity & justice, the South ought to have a fair proportion of the new territories & I have therefore, was been & still am an advocate of the Missouri Compromise.

But what is now the state of affairs? Our friend Foote, from the commencement of the Session has been urging the appointment of the Committee. The vowed object was to obtain such a report as has been made. Non-intervention — the Nicholson letter has been the cry from the South. The speeches made in favor of this policy have been lauded to the echo of Southern men & the Southern press. In this state of changes, the Democracy of the North have moved in favor of what they believed & I had a right to believe to the Southern platform. The Missouri Compromise, — any interference with slavery in the territories on the part of Congress, was denounced as unconstitutional both by Mr. Calhoun & Cap for opposite reasons to be sure, but they united in the same result. It is now too late, I honestly believe, to induce the Democracy of the North to remove from the platform on which they stand. Had the South at the commencement of the Session, gone for the Missouri Compromise through to the Pacific, the Democracy, at least in Pennsylvania, would have as freely sustained the measure as they have done Non-Intervention. The Whig Party in Pennsylvania will go for Old Zach's Platform of Non Intervention. Neither Clay nor Webster has much influence with them & what is the difference between the President's non intervention & our non intervention? Only this: The President will not provide even a territorial Government whilst we prepare to do this; but so far as regards slavery, the two plans are precisely the same.

The South occupy a much weaker position in the North than they did three months ago. The project of the Nashville Convention, & by exhibiting such a division of opinion in the South, has quieted in a considerable degree the apprehensions of the North in regard to disunion.

California is greatly too large for a single State; & no person would have through of admitting her as such, had it not been for the Slavery question. Her sea coast embraces as many degrees latitude as that of Massachusetts, Rhode Island, Connecticut, New York, New Jersey, Delaware, Maryland, Virginia & North Carolina. Now what would be thought on this side of the Rocky Mountains of a State of such dimensions? California thus constituted would be an empire in herself. She may soon determine to become independent. The best security for her continuance in the Union is to divide her territory into two or more States, of a convenient size & thus create rival interests on the Pacific, which will render each portion more dependent upon the Federal Government. But perhaps a Southern man ought to reflect that every State which shall be carved out of California will eventually be a free State. Slite, If I were a member of the Senate, I would vote for & strenuously support Clemen's amendment running the Missouri Compromise through California as well as through the territories. I should do this especially, in regards to the latter if I were a Southern man; because of the doctrine of non intervention will be unsatisfactory & unpopular in the South within a brief period after it shall have been adopted. But above all, & first of all, at the expense of any political existence, I would adopt such a course as would preserve & harmonize the Union.

On the point, which you specially present, that of California having sent two members to the House of Representatives, without any previous enumeration of her inhabitants – I have not formed any decided opinion. This difficulty might be removed by allowing her one representative.

I have written you a long letter with which I am not pleased with myself, but shall send it for what it may be worth. I should be very glad indeed to see you & slite [sic] more so, if you would, bring Mrs. Ellis along. I hope she is more comfortably lodged & in better health than she was. My niece is here, & if she will come I shall send for Mrs. Platt. The best letter which I have ever written on the Slave question & in favor of the Missouri Compromise will now probably never see the light.

Ever your friend,
James Buchanan

HL

Wheatland, 18 January 1850[124]
My dear Sir, [William R. King]
I did not mean, in anything I said in my former letter to insinuate that you would not stand by me when right with all the firmings of friendship. Such a thought never entered my mind.
....
In the Pennsylvanian to day I observed with astonishment a statement by Mr. Smith that "it would be found that the proclamation of

General Riley under which the Constitutional Convention of California had been organized & had acted, was issued under orders & authority derived from the late administration & before General Riley had received any instructions whatever from the present Executive."

If this be true I am wholly ignorant of the fact. According to my best recollection General Riley was sent to California merely as a military commander whatever instructions were given were addressed to General Pessifor F. Smith. It has always been my impression that the latter was superceded by the present administration.

One thing, however, is certain, that as Secretary of State, I addressed a letter to the agent of the Post Office Department sent out by Mr. Johnson with directions to have it published giving advice to the people of California what course they ought to pursue under the existing circumstances. This letter was carefully considered by the Cabinet it was in perfect consistency with the principle which we had always maintained that the power of the President over the territory had ceased with the termination of war.

Unless I am egregiously mistaken in my memory this letter will prove directly the reverse of what Senator Smith has stated. I think the name of the individual to whom it was addressed is Voorkies; but of this I am not certain. The letter was recorded in the Domestic Letter Book. I have for months past been looking out for publication of that letter in some California Newspaper; but it has never to my knowledge made its appearance & I have sometimes suspected it was suppressed because it might have been an obstacle in the way of the new Constitution. Mr. Glopbrenner, the present Sergeant at arms of the House was the Clerk who kept the Domestic Letter Book.

According to my best recollection, this letter was written to do away the effect of a letter addressed by Col. Benton to the people of California & transmitted by Col. Fremont advising them to establish a Government for themselves. This letter of Col. B. published at the time of some of the Journals. So far as Col. Benton is concerned, however, I wish the communication to be confidential.

My letter was addressed momentarily to the Post Office agent sent out to California by the Postmaster General, whatever his name may be, but really to the people of California. The action of the last administration cannot be understood without the publication of this letter. It may be among the papers sent to the House; but this I exceedingly doubt.

I have communicated these facts, merely, that our friends may know the State of the case. Mr. Walker, the late Secretary of the Treasury, will recollect all about it. This letter was of a public character & there can be no secrecy concerning it. Unfortunately, I left the original draft of it in the Department or I would send it to you. If you communicate the substance of the letter to our friend Walker, it will refresh his memory.

From you friend
very respectfully
James Buchanan
P.S. I have been astonished that the letter written to California by Col. Benton has not been alluded to. I feel confident it was published in the New York Herald perhaps in the National Intelligencer.

Wheatland 15th March 1850[125]
My dear Sir, [William R. King]
I have just received the National Intelligencer of yesterday morning & in looking over the proceedings of the Senate, I find that Mr. Seward said. — "I think it was Jefferson who said that the natural ally of Slavery in the South was the Democracy of the North

Mr. Hale. It was Buchanan who said so." —

Now, I have been greatly injured by the circulation of brief short sentences falsely attributed to me, witness the drop of blood lie, & I have no doubt unless this is just to rest on the floor of the Senate, the abolition & free soil papers of the North will have this sentence placarded in all their papers.

The natural ally of Slavery in the South is the Democracy of the North" —

James Buchanan.

General Cap & Mr. Foote were very ready to defend Mr. Jefferson but did not say a word about your absent friend.

The only observation which according to my best recollection which I ever made that would give the least color to such an interpretation is to be found in my speech on the veto power delivered in the Senate of the United States of the United States on the 2nd February 1842, reported in the appendix to the Congressional Globe for the year page 133. The particular portion of this speech to which I refer you will find in page 137. It begins with the following sentence: — Let me suppose another case of much more "dangerous character."

I shall very happily indeed to have the whole of the paragraph read. I don't retract a word of it; but glory in it. This however, affords no foundation for the charge.

I may have said upon other occasions in the Senate, for I have often said [in] conversation, that beyond the limit of the Slave States themselves, the Slaveholders have no friend or allies to stand by their Constitutional rights except the Democracy of the North. This is true to the letter & has been true for many years.

You might discover to what speech of mine Hale refers. I have no fear that he can show any such excerption of mine any where.

I am sorry to give you this trouble but to whom else can I refer to just [sic] me right by yourself?

From your friend
very respectfully,
James Buchanan

P.S. If you choose, please show this letter to Col. Davis. I know he would always be willing to defend an absent friend.

Wheatland 12th October 1850[126]
My dear Harriet,

Mr. McSwain of Philadelphia, with whom I had contracted to put up a furnace & kitchen range this week has disappointed me & I cannot leave home until this work shall be finished. He writes me that he will certainly commence on Monday morning; if it is so, I hope to be in New York the beginning of the week after, say bout the 22 Instant.

You ask what about your staying at Miss Bancroft's? With this I should be very much pleased, but it seems from your letter that she did not ask you to do so. She wished "to see a great deal" of you when you come to New York, implying that you were not to stay with her all the time. If she has since given you the invitation, <u>accept it.</u>

Could I have anticipated that you would not pass some time at Governor Marcy's, I should have arranged this matter by writing to Miss Bancroft. It is now too late.

I may probably pass a few days at the Aster House in New York, but I may have to see so many politicians, that I should have but little time to devote to you. I desire very much to reach New York before the departure of Miss Slidell which will be on the 26th Instant.

I shall be very glad if Clem Pleasonton should accompany you home; though the leaves are beginning to change color & to fall.

I have received a letter from Mary. From it, I doubt whether she will leave Jessie until the Spring. Without her, she does not perceive how Jessie can get along at house-keeping this winter. Mary is much pleased with Washington. Many of the ladies have called upon her, — a contrast with Lancaster. Ere this I presume she has heard from her husband as I forwarded a letter to her postmarked at Stockton, California.

Professor Muhlenberg, having been appointed a professor in Pennsylvania College (Gettysburg) has ceased to teach school & James Henry left for Princeton on Thursday last.

We have no local news, at least I know of none that would interest you. I think we shall have very agreeable neighbours in the Garden at Abbeville. Please to remember me very kindly to Mr. & Mrs. Robinson & give my love to Rose.

Yours affectionately
James Buchanan

HL

Mr. J. M. Smith[127]
Wheatland, near Lancaster 6 August 1851
My dear Sir

On my return home after a fortnight's absence I found your favor of the first instant.

I regret very much that you did not receive my order for a Refrigerator. It was sent to you immediately after the publication of a sketch of your biography with the Atlas: and I presumed as the money was not forwarded for want of a knowledge of the price, that you might have been unwilling to forward the article to a stranger. The season is now considerably advanced, I can very well do with what I have until another year, especially as I shall be from home much of the time between this & October.

Yours very respectfully
James Buchanan

HL

Saratoga Springs, 8 August 1852[128]
My dear Harriet

I arrived at this place on Thursday evening last & now on Sunday morning before Church am addressing you this note from Mrs. Plitt soon. I find the Springs very agreeable & the company very pleasant; yet there does not appear to be so many of the "dashers" here as I have seen. The crowd is very great in fact it is quite a mob of fashionable folks. Mrs. Plitt is very agreeable & quite popular. Mrs. Slidell is the most gay, brilliant, & fashionable lady at the Springs; as I am her admirer & attached to her party I am thus rendered a little more conspicuous in the beau monde than I could desire. Mrs. Rush conducts herself very much like a lady & is quite popular. She has invited me to accompany her to Albinis concert tomorrow evening, I would rather go with her to any other place. Albini is the rage here. I have seen him converse with her, am rather suspect in her favor. She is short & thick, but has a very good, arch & benevolent countenance. I shall, however, soon get tired of this place, do not expect to remain here longer than next Thursday. Not having heard from you, I should have felt somewhat uneasy; had Mary not written to Mrs. Plitt. I expect to be at home in two weeks from the time I started. Mrs. Plitt desires me to send her love to you & Miss Hetty. Remember me affectionately to Miss Hetty and James Henry & believe me to be

    Yours affectionately,
    James Buchanan

HL

Wheatland, near Lancaster 15 March 1853[129]
My dear Harriet,

I received yours of the 11th postmarked the 14th last night. I now receive about fifty letters per day, last Saturday 69; the cry is still they come, so that I must be brief. I labor day and night.

You ask: Will you accept the mission to England? I answer, that it has not been offered, I have not the least reason to believe from any authoritive [sic] source that it will be offered. Indeed, I am almost certain that it will not because surely General Pierce would not nominate one to the Senate without first asking one whether I would accept. Shall the offer be made, I know not what I might conclude. Personally, I have not the least desire to go abroad as a foreign minister. But "sufficient unto the day is the evil thereof." I really would not know where to leave you, were I to accept a foreign mission, & this would be one serious objection.

I think you are wise in going to Miss Macalester's. You know how much I esteem & admire Mrs. Tyler; but such a long visit to a friend is often a great bore. Never make people twice glad. I have not seen Kate Reynolds since her return, I have had no time to see any person.

In remarking as I did upon your composition, I was far from intending to convey the idea that you should write your letters as you would a formal address. Stiffness in a letter is intolerable. Its perfection is to write as you would converse. Still all this may be done with correctness. Your ideas are well expressed & the principle fault I found was in your not forming distinct periods. — or full stops, as the old schoolmaster used to say. Miss Word's letters are probably written with too much care, — too much precision.

We have not news. We are jogging on in the old John Trot style & get along in great peace & harmony.

    Yours affectionately
    James Buchanan

HL

Wheaton near Lancaster 19 March 1853[130]

My dear Harriet,

I return you Mrs. Crosby's appeal so that you have know it before you are preparing your answer. The whole matter is supremely ridiculous. I have no more reason to believe than I had when I last wrote, that I shall be offered the mission to England. Should the offer be made, it will be a matter of grave and serious consideration whether I shall accept or decline it. I have not determined this answer. "Sufficient unto the day is the evil thereof." Should it be accepted, it will be in the express conditions that I shall have liberty to choose my own Secretary of Legation; & from the specimen of diplomacy whether Mr. Crosby has presented, I think I may venture to say he will not be the man. I would secure some able industrious hardworking friend in whose integrity & providence I could place entire reliance. In fact, I have the man now in my eye from a distant State, to whom I would make the offer, — a gentleman trained by myself in the State Department. I must have a man of business & not a careful thought, who would go abroad to cut a dash.

Now you may say to Mr. Crosby that you believe I know nothing of the intervention of the President to offer me this English mission, that you are equally ignorant whether I would accept or decline it (& this you may say with truth for I do not know myself.) If accepted, however, you presume that I would cast about among my numerous friends for the best man for the appointment; & whatever your own wishes might by, you would not venture to interfere in the matter. That you took no part in such matters, This ought to be the substance of your letter, whether you may smooth over with as many honeyed phrases as you please.

I think that a visit to Europe, with me as minister would spoil you outright. Besides it would consume your little independence. One grave objection to my acceptance of the mission, for whether I have no personal inclination, would be your situation. I should dislike to leave you behind in the care of any person I know.

I think there is a decided improvement in your last letter. Your great fault was that your sentences run into each other without proper periods.

Good night! I cannot say how many letters I have written to day. Thank Heaven! Tomorrow will be a day of rest. I do not now expect to visit Pittsburgh until after the first of April, though I have a pecuniary concern of some importance.

With my kindness & regards to Miss Macalester, the family, I remain yours affectionately,

James Buchanan

ℋℒ

Washington, March 19th 1853[131]
Dear Sir, [James Buchanan]
I must leave to "expresseno silence" our emotions of gratitude.

The letter addressed to Mr. K. has been <u>disposed</u> of according to your <u>directions</u>. So soon as an opportunity presents, I shall pay my respects to the gentleman you refer me to.

The appeal you make must be gratified. Should it be refused, you may readily imagine the cause.

Our expectations of liquidating our primary obligations soon, are <u>uptodate bright</u>. God knows what a day may bring forth.

Very truly,
Your obedient friend
M. M. King

P.S. Truly do we feel the absence of Col. King, and deeply lament the cause of it. There is great comfort however in the reflection that Almighty God has timely admonished him of this approaching end and had protracted the catastrophe; thereby offering ample time for hallowed communings and fearful submissions to a dearer which affect all alike.

ℋℒ

LETTER NOT SENT
Wheatland, near Lancaster 2 April 1853[132]
My dear Sir, [Franklin Pierce]
Whilst I feel much honored by your kind & complimentary offer to appoint me Minister to England, I regret that recent events have placed its acceptance beyond my power.

Amidst all your appointments for Pennsylvania you have not in the exercise of your discretion selected a single individual whom I had recommended for any particular office. No, not one. Whilst I feel proudly conscious that I recommended no friend whom I did not believe to be the best, most popular, & most deserving man for the places & yet was not to unreasonable as to expect that you would appoint all or a majority of such friends. I trust that experience has taught me how to appreciate the delicacy & perplexity of your situation; & therefore I indulged no such expectations. Had you appointed even a single individual of my selection, I should have taken your highly flattering offer, into serious consideration & have been governed in my decision by a sense of duty to the Country & to your administration. As it is, I could not now accept the mission without subjecting myself to the imputation, however, unjustly, of having selfishly received it as an equivalent for the disappointment of all my friends. Besides, my acceptance of it would necessarily blast the expectations of other friends in Pennsylvania who yet indulge the hope that they may be appointed to foreign missions. In my public career, I have always endeavored to be not only chaste but unsuspected.

I can assure you that I write in no callous or unfriendly spirit. I trust I know how to discriminate between the public acts of an administration & the personal predilections of its head. As a private citizen, your administration will receive my decided support, as long as it shall carry out in practice the principles presented with so much eloquence & ability in your excellent inaugural address; & judging from your past character, I feel entire confidence that these principles will be your constant guide.

As I feel no hesitation in declining the mission, I answer by the returning mail so as to enable you to submit some other name to the Senate; because I believe that the sanction of the Senate contributes so little to the estimation in which the minister is held abroad.

Yours very respectfully
James Buchanan

HL

LETTER SENT
To: His Excellency Franklin Pierce[133]
Wheatland, near Lancaster 2 April 1853
My dear Sir,

I have received & hasten to answer your favor of the 30th ultimo, expressing your determination to tender me the Mission to England, as soon as you shall be advised as to what will serve my convenience in point of time. For this distinguished & gratifying evidence of your regard, communicates in terms so kind & acceptable, I shall be equally indebted, whether it is accepted or declined. If accepted, I could not without great personal inconvenience & pecuniary loss, leave the county before the month of June.

I shall advise you of my decision at earliest practicable moment; & in the mean time, believe me to be very gratefully & respectfully

Your friend
James Buchanan

HL

Private & Confidential[134]
Lancaster 7 April 1853
My dear Harriet,

I am thus far on my way to Washington, wholly uncertain whether I shall accept or decline the mission. This will depend upon circumstances which I cannot know until after my arrival in the city. I have not the least personal inclination to go abroad. Your letter was highly gratifying to me. As soon as I shall have decided, I will inform you of it.

In haste, your affectionately
James Buchanan

HL

Wheatland July 14 1853[135]
My dear Lily,

Your truly gratifying epistle was received by us whilst taking a most romantic stroll with the fair and fragile Amos S. —your expressions of tenderness served as a balm to any wounded spirits where upon I indulged in the luxury of a laugh. Which luxury I had been most barbarously and unjustly despaired of, by the tearing asunder of certain tender bias, by two kind damsels—forsaking me at a time when loneliness only was my portion. You are all alone at Louisdale, and I alone at Wheatland. Idol of my heart!! Stronghold of my affections! Why is it fate deals so harshly with us? Have we dove ought to visit such treatment? - alas! Us the innocent suffer with the guilty. I must rouse my philosophy and submit. — Thank you from my heart my own "drooping Lily" for your wishes to see me at Louisdale — my spirit is ever with you but the body can emigrate is beyond my powers of clairvoyance to fix upon decidedly. Mary and Mr. Neil are doubtless with you now, and I cannot feather myself so much and to think — with other powerful attractions I will be so much missed. I have faithfully and religiously delivered all your tender conjurements to my much honored Uncle — he was much pleased, and sends you a perfect heart consider in reply — he says "my love to Miss Lily, and tell her if her lands were not worth a cent (one cent I would think more highly of her if possible) than I do at present." You are fortunate my disinterested friend — you receive some replies to your boring suggestions — more fortunate than some of your friends, who have to submit to its being entirely a one sided affair, in the way of messages — ahem!!! Uncle was in Philadelphia but for a day — I was truly glad to his return as Miss Hetty left yesterday morning to accompany Mrs. Weaver and her children to Washington — so that I was entirely alone — but my good, dear Uncle, did not forget me in my loneliness — but returned to cheer his loved one. He has not yet fixed the day for his departure for England. Your friend Mr. Lightner was here this morning making many inquires for the "absent ladies" — as usual I made a mail-

agent of him. During Miss Hetty's absence the housekeeping duties devolve upon me — I hope to acquit myself honorably as the distinguished degree is only conferred upon me until Saturday or Monday. Lydie's movements puzzled me as much as they possibly could have done you. — James wrote me "Lyddie has gone" — but the idea was so appalling to him that he could not take me where she had gone — several days after I received a letter from Pittsburgh without any name annexed; but from the contents handwriting etc., I judged Miss Speer was the composer — and immediately set down both individuals as having arrived at that state when neither, were in any way, accountable for their own actions. <u>Have you ever been in that situation ???</u> Jim Reynolds has been out several times since your departure and I have failed to excite a little curiosity in your behalf. I told Kate of the summary manner in which we had disposed of her family. She seemed quite well phased. Last night after Uncle's return we regaled ourselves with the highly intellectual amusement of shooting owls and in our eagerness dispatched these — and as Uncle has "placed a price upon their heads." I imagine many more will share the fate of their mangled companions. I called to see the Misses Porter last week, but to my disappointment found they had left for Easton and parts unknown, & for a time indefinite. Your lover will be true to his promise about the daguerreotype — my Uncle understands his duty. ahem!!! I hope you will appreciate the exertion I am making in your behalf this after noon — for you know of old my aversion to letter writing after dinner — The task has been to me an agreeable one, and if it gives you any pleasure, dear Lily, I am amply repaid — but if you find [me] dull and stupid — this time, at last I have an apology. Mrs. Danforth's letter has never yet been dispatched — but if she is away from home, it is of no importance. I receive very cheering and tender intimations of William R.'s fidelity. My sister in law is still on Staten Island. When do you go to Chicago? — Farewell, thou consumer of my hearts best affections and let her who feeds upon thy every look, hear cheering and loving words of consolations from thee: and that right speedily. Love to all ever and as ever, your own,
'Henriqueta'

Astor House, New York 4 August 1853[136]
My dear Harriet
John Van Buren called to see me this morning & was particularly amiable. He talked much of what his father had written & said to him respecting yourself, expressed great desire to see you, we talked much about you. He intimated that his father had aroused him to address

you. I told him he would make for me a very rebellious nephew & would be hard to manage.

He asked where you would be this winter. I told him you would be visiting your relatives in Virginia in the frame of a month & might probably come to London next Spring or Summer. He said he would certainly see you & asked for a letter of introduction to you which I promised to give him. As he was leaving, he told me not to forget it but give it to the proprietor of the Astor House before I left & I promised to do so. I told him that you had appreciated his father's kindness to you felt honored & grateful for his attentions, admired him very much. He knew all about your pleasant interview with his father in Philadelphia. There was much other talk which I consider & still consider to be bagatelle yet the subject was pursued by him. As I have a leisure moment I thought that I would propose you for an interview with him in case you should meet.

John Van Buren is a man of ease abilities & great wit & is quite successful in his profession. His political cause has been eccentric but he still maintains his influence. I never saw him look so well as he did to day. I respect that I believe all this to be bagatelle, yet it seemed to be mingled with a strong desire to see you.

Saturday morning 6 Aug;— I passed an hour last evening with Mrs. Sickles. She is both handsome & agreeable. And, now, my dear Harriet, with the blessings of God, I shall go aboard the Atlantic this morning with a firm determination to do my duty, without any unpleasant apprehensions of the result. Relying upon that gracious being who has protected me all my life until the present ... I go aboard once more in the service of my country, with fair hopes of success. I shall drop you a line from Liverpool, immediately upon my arrival.

With my kindest regards for Miss Hetty I remain
Yours affectionately
James Buchanan

HL

Clarendon Hotel, London 15 September 1853[137]
My dear Harriet,
On the day before yesterday I received your kind letter of the 28 August with a letter from Mary which I have already considered. How rejoiced I am that she is content & happy in San Francisco. I also received your favor of the 18 August in due time. I write you this evening; because I have important dispatches to prepare for the Department tomorrow to be sent by Saturday's steamer.

How rejoiced I am that you did not come with me! Perceiving your anxiety, I was several times on the point of saying to you come along; but you would see as much fashionable society at Wheatland as you would see here until February or March next. You cannot conceive how dull it is; although personally I am content. The beau monde are all at their country seats or on the Continent there to remain until the meeting of Parliament. But what is worse than all, I have not yet been able to procure a home in which I would consider to live. I have looked at a great many.— The houses of the nobility & gentry, but the furnishings in all of them is old decayed & wretched, & with very few exceptions, they are <u>very very dirty.</u> I can account for this in no other manner than that they are not willing to rent them until the furniture is worn out & that London is for them like a great watering place from about the first of March until the first of August. This hotel which is the most fashionable in London is not nearly equal to the first hotels in Philadelphia & New York; & yet the cost of living at it with two rooms & a chamber is about $90 per week. The enormous expense & the superior attractions drive all the American travelers to Paris and the Continent. The London Times has taken up the subject & is now daily comparing the superior cheapness & superior accommodations of the Hotels in the United States with theirs in London. Here there are as lable d'hotels of the houre may be full without your knowing who is in it. I think I have the treasure in a servant (Jackson), I brought with me from New York. If he should only hold out, he is all I could desire.

Mr. Walsh my expectations as a man of business. Col. Lawrence the attaché without is industrious, gentlemanly & has been highly useful. He knows every body & works as though he received $10,000 per annum. I venture to say as abled & useful a legation as any in London. Lawrence has gone to Scotland in the company with Miss Chapman & her father & I think he is much pleased with her. In truth she is a nice girl & very handsome. The Chapman's will return immediately to the United States.

[Lady] Willisby is suffering from the dropsy & she with her sister Lady Stafford, remained a few days at the house. I saw a good deal of them whilst they were here & they have been very kind to me. They love to talk about America & yet appear to have genuine American hearts. Lady Willisby lives at Hampton Court,— this old historic place about fifteen miles from London … I am going there to dine with them & see the palace on Saturday. I shall take Sickles and Walsh with me according to Lady Willisby's special request, though she does not know them.

Though these American girls have had a strange fate, many of their sex have cursed them, but I think without cause. They are all childless, would I verily believe have been more happy had they been united to independent intelligent gentlemen in their own country. It is impossible to conceive of a more elegant & accomplished lady than

Lady Willisby ..." [The remainder of this letter was damaged and illegible.]

HL

U.S. Legation[138]
London. May 4, 1854
I must write you, dear Lily,

Though, as yet I have not much of interest to relate, concerning myself. — I only arrived here on Saturday evening and until presented to the Queen, will not be fairly in the "London world." Everything is as comfortable and agreeable as possible, about my home — all things promise to me a pleasant visit. Uncle met me on the Ship at Liverpool & is looking remarkably well, & in good spirits — is as kind and good as possible & decidedly the most elegant looking man I have seen since I left home. My court-dress is now absorbing most of my attention, as I will be presented this day week (11th) — this is rather intense as I must act entirely for myself — with not the good taste of Mrs. Plitt to consult; whose kindness, at home, I always depended upon. I go to decide upon it today. Last evening we went to a Literary Club dinner — the ladies of course in the gallery. I was disappointed in the speaking — we had expected several distinguished speakers but only heard Lord Mahon, & Lord Stanley both men of talent. — Lord Mahon was the best speaker at the table — but he talked too much, and said too little. Lord Stanly talked a great deal, and said nothing. I was gratified to see the manner of conducting a public dinner here, but without doubt, our people are more prompt and eloquent — in fact, I have seen no improvements upon our country, except in servants, — here they are most respectful and respectable. Tonight I go to the Opera, with Mr. Peabody and a party he has formed for me — he is a younger looking man than I had expected to see, & seems very good and kind hearted. He made very particular inquires about your good Father. Tomorrow and Saturday I go to dinner parties, and I suppose will be fairly launched in the gay world, after next week.

I had a glimpse of the Queen yesterday — she held a Levee (gentleman alone) at St. James! Lady Oasily took me to the Park, where we had an excellent view of all the Royal procession. — The Life-guards are splendid looking men — mounted upon black horses — the Queen's band played — of course, I was very much entertained — but I could scarcely convince myself that it was the ruler of this great kingdom — approaching the glitter was so great it appeared like a grand show. From the carriage, she struck me as being handsome, but she is not generally considered so. Your friend Mr. Corbon is here from Paris — his stay will be short — he is to be here this morning. — Unfortunately I will not see him, as I am obliged to go out. You know Mr. Holford is dead.

You have heard, dear Lily, of our long & boisterous voyage — a fortnight reaching London. — I have not ceased to mourn over the pleasant evening, with you all, I was deprived of, when first we started. Friday 5. I was charmed at the Opera last night. Beethoven's Fidelio was the piece. I heard the great Cravelli, and think her superb — the music is grand & effective. Mr. Peabody's box is opposite the Queen's — she, Prince Albert, & two of the children were there. Mr. P. is very kind — he had a large party of Americans last evening — and seems ready to entertain any who come, give my warmest love to Dame Trip — tell her I read the little book every day, and think it sweet. I gaze upon my daguerreotypes with much tenderness, and is the kindness which gave them. Uncle is laboriously occupied writing all the time — in fact, too much confined. I hope you have written me, dear Lily, ere this — I will have the blues, if every steamer does not bring me some affectionate effusion and could you know the value of a jingle line, when so far separated from every home association, I know you would write often. I sincerely hope you safely recovered from your cold. My love to Mr. M. tell him the gingerbread was very acceptable. Love to grandma ... — and do write me often, dear Lily — I hope my next letter will be more interesting for you. I have no doubt Uncle would send some message — but as the dispatch lay very close — I cannot wait for any tender words interesting as I know they would be to you. If you see Mrs. Plitt tell her I am well — as I have not time to write her this mail. Love to every one & believe me ever dear Lily your sincerely affectionate Hattie.

Capt West is a glorious fellow - I [never met] a more agreeable escort.

Soldier's House Tuesday Sept. 13, 1857[139]
My dear Lily,

I had no idea you would write me from West Point, & therefore was not very much disappointed. I know how full of pleasure your visits are — how your hands are filled with pleasant duties — & how your eyes are dazzled with the glitter & glare of brass buttons & knowing all this, dear Lily, I really did not expect you to write. We all regret you could not pay us a visit here this summer — but as the Floyd's have been absent the entire season, you would not have enjoyed the country much. Mr. Floyd writes very cheerfully, but does not consider himself restored in health. Mrs. Floyd is far from well, & has been miserable all summer — they will return very soon. Washington has been shockingly dull this summer — a few foreigners were the only persons left in town. This last week has brought a few of the wanderers home. We are having delightful weather, & I enjoy my daily rides intensely — I have a nice little beau, always ready at my command. He lives close by, & you can imagine how charmingly convenient it is. We will return to town by the 1st of Oct. probably earlier; — The town looks so dusty & dirty, that I hate to think of it until the cold weather. Did I tell you that your chances were all over with Dr. King? & that he astonished us all this summer, by bringing home one fine day — a nouvelle mariée? You shall have your Army Register in a day or two.

I fear I cannot do more than I promised you in the spring dear Lily — & that is, to pass a few days with you, if you are still in the country when I go to Pennsylvania. You may be sure I will stay as long a possible. My "leave of absence" must be very short this Autumn. Miss Hetty is not coming to Washington until the winter. — James Henry is away, & when I leave, Uncle will be entirely alone — so I shall only be from home long enough to "rig up" for the winter & take a glimpse at some few friends. I must go to Lancaster — my brother has lost one of his children this Summer, & I feel it to be a duty to go see them — there are also other things that make it my duty to pass a few days in Lancaster this Autumn. We expect a visit from our old friend Sir H. Holland, whom I believe you know! He has no doubt arrived in the country, & expects to be here the last of the month.

Mr. & Mrs. Henry!!! were at Lake George when last I heard from them. They will pay a little visit to Annapolis, & these parts, & settle down in New York by the 1st. He is too happy to write — & advises every one "to go & do likewise." I am bound to believe what you say about the "Medico" — & if I find myself deceived, my faith in woman is forever gone. When is Sally Butler to be married? I hear Dr. Wistar was engaged to a lovely girl here, a Miss McKane, & that he heard some rumor about her family — (doubtless unfounded) — & broke the engagement. She has felt it very keenly ever since, for she was sincere. Sarah had better keep an eye to her lover.

Mrs. Plitt has returned to Philadelphia — & has been very ill within the last few weeks, but I trust she is quite well again. Give my love to your father. Write me, dear Lily, & be sure that I will see you some time this Autumn though my visit will not be as long as I should like it.

Believe me, always, dear Lily - Yours very affectionately
Harriet R. Lane

Excuse carelessness, as the postman is waiting — & there is no time "to review." What think you of Douglas' pronunciamento?!!!

May 20, 1858[140]

My dear Harriet

Learning that you were about to purchase furniture in New York, I requested Mr. Blake to furnish me a statement of the balance of the appropriation. ... The balance is $8,369.02. In making your purchases therefore, I wish you to consider that this sum must answer our purchases until the end of my term. I wish you therefore to not to expend the whole of it, but to leave enough to meet all contingencies until 4 March 1861. Any sum which may be expensed above the appropriations I shall most certainly pay out of my own pocket. I shall never ask Congress for the Deficiency.

Who should make the appearance this morning but Mr. Karth. After talking about other matters for some time he said he was married. I expressed strong doubts upon the subject when he insisted that he was actually, bona fide married. The lady is Miss Sparks whom he has been so long addressing.

With my kind regards to Mr. & Mrs. R., I remain yours

Affectionately

James Buchanan

HL

Washington[141]

May 5th 1860

My dear Miss Lane

If I were to invite you to dinner Monday or Wednesday next would you come and would Miss Macalester and Miss Buchanan accompany you?

Yours very truly

[Lord] Lyons

Accompanied an invitation for Wednesday May 9, 1860, 7:00 pm

HL

Letter Addressed to: Charles Macalester Esq. 205 S. 6th Street Philadelphia

The Executive Mansion Washington[142]

Friday May 11th, 1860

Your letter of yesterday with its enclosure my dear Father just received thanks for both I am sorry you had such unpleasant weather for your trip to New York. Did Commodore Stockton take his whole family with him? I was so shocked to hear of Dr. Henry's loss, it must have been a fearful blow to his poor wife, who was certainly devotedly attached to him. Dr. Jackson too is I fancy much grieved.

This has been a very gay week, the dinner at Lord Lyons' was charming, the table arrangements all very elegant the company consisting of 21 persons, very select & the host, Courteous gentlemanly and agreeable. He took Hattie to dinner & the Russian Minister took me & Commodore Tatnall Miss Buchanan. Gen. Scott was there, Vice President & Mrs. Breckinridge, the Spanish Minister & a number of distinguished persons. In the evening we went to a party given by Mrs. Lewis & Miss Taylor which was delightful, where we had a nice little dance. Last evening we were at a little company at Miss Wilson's & today we have a large dinner at home. Gen. Scott & his aide Col. Heyes, a most agreeable gentleman, Commodore Tatnall are among the expected guests, 36 in all. On Monday the Japanese, it is supposed will arrive, on Wednesday the President possibly will receive them, but the program has not been decided on. I will go keep you posted. Today we are going under escort of the "officers in charge" to see the suite of apartments prepared for them which are said to be splendid. The President thinks the Convention at Baltimore has made a great mistake in not nominating Gen. Houston who would have made a good man, Bell he does not consider a popular man & he told me what I never before heard that he drinks hard, did you know it? John Van Buren, was here for several days, & we saw a great deal of him, he is exceedingly agreeable & entertaining. He appears to admire Hattie greatly. He has been very sick & she thought he was looking very badly. A letter from Julia confirms your report as to the children's having whooping cough but the season is favorable & I hope they will have it lightly. I have been favored in the floral line lately, having received two lovely bouquets on Tuesday and another on Wednesday, one from Mr. Thompson, of Southampton (our Consul.) And two from Lieut. Michler of the Army. Love to Aunty & Brother & John, Mrs. Gilpin & the Gross'. Hattie sends love.

Yours, ever affectionately, Lily.-

Thanks to Mr. Ellis, for sending me the Papers'.-

P.S. - I send you the Constitution with Jefferson Davis' speech in full. Remember me to Annie & James. [Written across the top of the first page]

HL

Letter addressed to: Charles Macalester Esq. 205 S 6th Street Philadelphia

Executive Mansion[143]

May 13th, 1860

My dear Father,

I wrote you quite a lengthy epistle on Friday, and now merely wish to send a few lines to show that I am always thinking of you, amid all my enjoyments. The large dinner on the day I wrote, was charming. The guests were 36 in number among them Gen. Scott in full uniform, gorgeous, & dazzling to behold, [Chapean] Sword & all complete! After the company had dispersed the President went up to smoke a cigar in his office, & I with him, for a chat. I told him he would have to get up some sort of uniform in which to receive the Japanese, or they certainly would mistake Gen. Scott for the great man of the nation. He laughed, & said "well I have a dressing gown that Gen. Harney gave me, perhaps that would do, but afterwards concluded, that for him to be in plain black in the midst of all the uniforms would show them that-simplicity was a mark of distinction in this Country. I enclose you today's "Constitution" with pretty sharp notice of Mr. Ingersoll's speech, which it merited, how in the world could he have been guilty of such bad taste? We are all surprised at Mr. Everett's accepting the Nomination for Vice President. The Post Master at New York, Mr. Fowler, has been discovered to be a defaulter to the amount of one hundred and fifty-six thousand dollars, & the Post-office there was yesterday placed in the hands of The Federal Government agents, sent on for the purpose. The President & Mr. Holt are greatly displeased about it. Your friend Steinberger is here trying for the mission to Guatemala & is strongly backed by Gen. Lane, but he will not get it. Emily Padnalader & Mr. & Mrs. George Blight were at Hattie's reception yesterday. They are all staying with Mrs. Palmer. Emily looks wretchedly. Mrs. Clay was also here & asked for you very kindly as did also Mr. Taylor & others. Col. Hardee arrived on Friday & looks remarkably well, he is coming to go to church with me this morning. To show how hurried Mr. Buchanan is, all the time as soon as I mentioned on Friday evening, that I had a visit from my friend Col. Hardee that morning he said, "Well you must ask him to come & take a family dinner with us, & we will invite Gen. Johnston, who has just arrived too." My package by express came safely to hand on Friday, thanks for the same to you & Aunty & Annie, as all I believe had a hand in dispatching it. Hattie desires much love, yours ever most affectionately,
Lily L. Macalester.
P.S. Love to all the family.

HL

Letter sent to: Charles Macalester Esq. 205 S 6th Street Philadelphia.
Executive Mansion Washington[144]
Friday May 25th 1860

Nothing from you my dearest Father since Tuesday, but a letter received this morning from Puss Gross assures me that you are well, & that she & Lon dined with Brother Shields & yourself on Wednesday. I was delighted to find that you had been so well entertained. — Madame De Limbourg's Matinee which I wrote you was to come on Tuesday, was really charming & elegant. The garden which is very pretty, was thrown open & beautifully fixed up, a tent at one end had ices, & strawberries, & an area was lined (the brick walls) with bright chintz & filled with Lounges, chairs & etc. ... a table on one side with punch cakes etc. — The substantials were on a table elegantly "Spread out" in the dinning room. The house is double & the dancing was in the back parlor, it was altogether, one of the most charming, & brilliant parties I have ever attended. The Japanese appeared much pleased with everything. The young prince with whom I had a small flirtation by the aid of dumb motions & my opera glass (which I showed him how to use) on Saturday recognized me most [flatteringly] & really was quite animated in his expressions of satisfaction. The others made solemn, & dignified bows to both Hattie & I. — Today the grand dinner comes off & he is to take me to table. Hattie is to be seated between two, & declares that I shall be, but I am petitioning for "A Native American," on one side of me, She vows. I shall have two Japanese & so the war is raging; how we will settle it remains to be seen. I will write you an account of the dinner, which will I am sure be very amusing. We suggested to Mr. Buchanan that it would be considered a mark of distinction by the Ambassadors, if they were placed on either side of him at the table, whereupon he threw up his hands & exclaimed, "that he would not be paid to do it," so he will be quietly ensconced as usual between two agreeable ladies whilst Hattie & I entertain the ambassadors. — Mr. Buchanan is very anxious to procure some good champagne, & I said he would get you to buy some for him, as he is not satisfied with what he finds in Washington & as his birthday came a short time since, & he reproached me laughingly with not making him a present. I wish you would send him a dozen bottles in a basket & if he likes it he can order more. I think it would please him & he is so kind, & so devoted to me, always doing, & saying something gratifying & flattering. He speaks of you constantly in the most complimentary, & really affectionate manner.

When any visitor asks me about my leaving, he hushes them, & me right up with "She is not going for some time. I cannot possibly get along without her so that is fixed, her Father has her all the time & can very well spare her to me for this little while, when I so want her." — Hattie desires her love, & tells me to say, that in your letter you consented to my staying a month longer, & that she shall consider you professions as "empty nothings," if you violate that promise; but that at all events you are not to come for me until tomorrow (Saturday) week &

then you are to come here & stay until Monday.— That she will be seriously displeased if you dare to come earlier, I am however at your disposal dear Father any day after Wednesday. On Tuesday Madam Bodisco's wedding comes off & on Wednesday, we have music on the grounds, which is perfectly lovely. Please bring a large hunk with you, as I have all my winter furs besides the additional dresses sent me, & want you to carry some of them home.

Best love to all from your most affectionately,
Lily
P.S.—Hattie sends you a flower how tender! It means preference.
This is the 4h letter I have written you this week. [written across the side of the first page]
Best love to all from yours most affectionately, Lily.-

Letter sent to: Charles Macalester Esq. 205 S. 6th Street
The Executive Mansion[145]
Saturday May 26th 1860
Your letter of the 24th arrived last evening dear Father, & by it I was amazed to find that you were going to Chicago as it was the first intimation you had given of such a plan. I shall of course be ready to return with you any day to Philadelphia although I hope I can be at Madame Bodisco's wedding, on Tuesday & remain until Wednesday. I hope you did not send James & the horses up to Lewisdale today, as I certainly shall want them very much after I return; do you suppose after sojourning in the Executive Mansion for two months, & dashing about — all the time in the President's Carriage, I can bring myself down suddenly to the humiliation of walking the streets of Philadelphia? I will soon get James back into his old habits of goodness, but pray do not send him up for Brothers management when neither you nor I, are there.— This of course between ourselves. The grand dinner to the Japanese came off yesterday & was a great success. The great Treasurer, Moruta Okatara took me to the table & the Prince Stkaharo Jugoro, sat on my left, three others were arranged along the end of the table who it also fell to my lot to entertain. So that I was talking, & motioning to five men, all through the dinner, not one of whom could speak a word of English.— The Interpreter came up every little while, & I made him convey ideas which I carried out by looks, & signs. I several times had the whole of them laughing heartily. The President complimented me extravagantly afterwards, & said "it was the most remarkable exhibition he had ever witnessed, & that he thought no other woman in the United States could have accomplished it successfully." Was that not a pretty compliment. They brought Hattie, Miss Buchanan, and I, each a present

consisting of an elegant box, containing, every variety of Japanese nick nacks, & several yards of handsome silk, which will certainly be always a very agreeable souvenir of their visit. — They are a dignified well bred people, & show marvelous tact in conforming to our usages. My friend the young Prince Stkahara Jugoro, is very bright, & interesting, asked me for my card, & to write my name on it, & then gave me his, complimented me through the Interpreter on my dancing at the Dutch Minister's, & altogether, we had quite a little flirtation. — He is a son of the richest man in Japan. — Sunday morning. — Your letter of yesterday dearest Father just received, & Hattie is sitting by me to send you a message, it is "her love, & thanks for the butter," which she greatly appreciated. She has a great deal to say to you about other interests, but expecting to see you so soon, she will not write, but convey her sentiments by word of mouth, and eyes. — She wishes you to come on here. Saturday, & stay until Monday, when you can take the Baltimore & Ohio road, at the Relay House, for Chicago & be so far on your way, & that I can return next week. This is Hattie's plan, mine is however for you to come down on Wednesday, & I will return with you on Thursday or Friday, as I think I ought to be at home, while you are gone, although Sophie & Annie are perfectly reliable, still I am sure you will be better satisfied, to leave if I am at home, & you have been so kind & so unselfish about my visit here, letting one have the full enjoyment of it, that I do not wish there should be a draw back to the satisfaction of your trip. — How long do you expect to be gone? & what has so suddenly determined you to go? Write & say what day we may expect you here, & believe me — yours' ever lovingly,

Lily

P.S. Love to all- [written across the side of the last page]

Letter sent to: Charles Macalester Esq. 205 S. 6th Street
Tuesday, May 29th 1860[146]
Executive Mansion

Yours of yesterday dearest Father just received & before making my toilette for The Wedding, I hasten to acknowledge it. — The President is to give away "the fat widow," & we have had a great deal of fun with him about it as for "wanting her himself," that is, as you imagined utterly absurd: he heard that she had said so, & was highly amused. She is a character, & very entertaining, she took tea here on Sunday evening & was full of news & gossip as usual. The wedding is at 12 no. & at 5 Mrs. Sidell has a so called Matinee, which will be, it is said, the most elegant affair given in Washington in a long while. The grounds are to be beautifully fitted up & her house is very handsome, dancing in drawing rooms. — I wish you were here to go to it. — Yesterday we drove to Arlington, Mrs. Mason you friend made up a party for me & it was charming. It is a grand old place, full of interesting relics & associations. Have you ever visited it. Hattie desires me to give her love & say "that she is indignant that you took no notice of her message to you she does not understand such treatment." — Let me know what day to expect you & I think your trunk will answer my purpose. I am delighted to hear that you have found a house, & much indebted to you for acceding to my request to keep them in town until my return. — Mrs. Nilling I dare say, feels relieved at Mr. Schott's death, you will have to be discrete now about visiting her. The butter kettles are safe & I will look after the cloths if possible, or rather direct Eliza to. — I understand Lincoln's nomination disquieted Douglas much, strange to say I have seen him but once, & then at a distance since I have been here, but I always speak of him in terms of personal kindness to everyone.— I will try to write Aunty by this evenings mail if possible, should I not accomplish it she must remember how much my time is engaged & pardon me. Your letters fill up all the vacant moments: I wrote you five times last week. — A note from Isabel received last evening gives a glowing recount of your dinner with which she was charmed. Love to all.

Yours ever affectionately
Lily

HL

Letter sent to: Mrs. Laftop 249 S 13th Street Philadelphia
Executive Mansion[147]
May 30th 1860

Your welcome note my dear Aunty should have been earlier answered, but that this last week has been filled up by incessant engagements, so as to leave me hardly a spare moment. Yesterday morning we attended Madam Bodisco's wedding, which was crowded with all the elite of Washington. The ceremony was performed in St. John's Church& the bride was dressed in a most exquisite violet colored silk, with three superb point d' Aleuson lace flounces, a white & lilac hat, & point lace mantle. It was a perfect toilette, & she looked very handsome in the face, but is enormous in figure. The groom was in full English Uniform, & a slight graceful young man.— At 6 in the afternoon we went to a party at Mrs. Slidell's which continued until eleven: one of the handsomest entertainments I have ever attended. Her house is very elegant & her grounds, & Mr. Corcoran's adjoining, were connected by a bridge beautifully festooned with Japanese & American flags, & cozy little summer houses, & tents with refreshments, scattered in all directions.— The dancing, was in the drawing rooms. At dusk the grounds were brilliantly illuminated with different colored lanterns, & as it was bright moonlight too really it looked like a fairy scene.— The Japanese appeared to enjoy it immensely. I had an ecstatic time, danced to my hearts content, strolled in the moonlight, and — but it is not worth while to go into details, only I am too sorry it is over.— I was glad to learn from Father's letter that Flora was with you, I hope she will stay until I return. Did she bring little Dick? Give her my best love, & say that I am anticipating great pleasure in seeing her again. I hope your present — guests will not interfere with your plan of receiving the Japanese, as I mentioned your hospitable intention , to Capt Lee, one of the Naval officers in charge of them & he was quite delighted, & accepted for them on the spot so you are fully committed.— I suppose you are almost residing at the Convention. Do no dissipate too much. Hattie has been shouting to me for a half hour to go into her room, & lie down a little while before dinner, as this is Music afternoon, & we have to be out on the Piazza & in the grounds until dark, so good bye.— Thanks for your suggestion that my friends must be tired of me. Hattie was indignant enough at it. They evince very opposite symptoms, I assure you, & will not let me speak of leaving, I shall however return with Father whom I am expecting this week.— I will have so much to talk about, when I reach home that I shall hardly take time to breathe for a week.

Love to all, yours ever affectionately

Lily-

Hattie's best love. The President was quite pleased at your message.

HL

Washington City

March 11, 1861

Miss Lane

The enclosed from the [Washington] Star will give you a pretty correct idea of the first reception of the new President. The only ladies present who visited you socially were Mrs. Palmer, Mrs. Franklin, Mrs. Magruder, Miss Mulberry, the Lorings, Miss Johnson and the younger Miss Pleasonton. The great mass of the crowd consorted with strangers and the remainder, mostly of citizens who have not been in the habit of being present on such occasions. When Mr. and Mrs. Lincoln entered the ball room, followed by the rest of their family, you can well imagine my surprise on seeing Professor McLeod in the retinue with Mrs. Edward on his arm. I am aware of the good lady had been aware that he had buried his wife so recently as within the last eight or nine days she would not have extended to him such a courtesy.

To be seen mingling in such a gay crowd under an affliction usually deemed the most painful evidence within a want of sense or heart.

...

Some of the incidents of the evening are worth relating. The house was not relieved of the crowds until near twelve o'clock.

Very respectively

Dr. Blake

H L

Head Quarters Army Corps[148]

Fort Monroe, Va. 8, Sept. 1862

My dear Miss Lane,

I have not forgotten that you sent me a letter for your friend Miss Ellis, which under rigor of military discipline I was constrained to return to you. I am now in a position to obey any command you may have without being overruled by superior authority.

Pray do not thing there is any latent selfishness in this outward profession of service. But if there were, if after several months of station here without hearing a word, directly or indirectly from Mr. Buchanan or from you yourself, while the remembrance of your kindness is ever fresh in my mind, I were greatly of the desire to hear that you both are well, would it not be a pardonable weakness?

With my kind regards taken,

I am very sincerely and respectfully yours

[General] John A. Dix

H L

Fort Monroe[149]

27 Sept. 1862

My dear Miss Lane

Your note came a few minutes ago, and write this promptly to say that I am sending a flag of truce up the James River today. Your letter to Mrs. Ellis will go with it to Richmond when it will take the further mail.

It was very pleasant to hear from you and Mr. Buchanan, to know that you are both well, I am happy as one can be in these unhappy times.

...

If I can do anything for your, please command my services with the assurance that in doing so you will afford me a sincere pleasure.

With my kindest regards to Mr. Buchanan.
I am very respectfully and sincerely yours,
[General] John A. Dix

HL

Camden[150]
April 13th 1866
[To Harriet Lane Johnston]
By a happy chance the cards with your new name found me at last, and although I had heard of you marriage, the reality of the event impresses me deeply. I have and do wish you every blessing for this life and greater blessings hereafter. My congratulations shall not be mired with any mention of the past for years four years. I expect to spend the summer in Camden, and propose an opportunity to meet you again. How much I shall have to ask, how much to tell. Present me to your husband and believe me that I love you as I ever did.
Your friend sincerely
Catherine M. Ellis

HL

June 10th 1866[151]
My dearest Hattie
I would long since have written a reply to your kind letter, and to offer you my most affectionate and heartfelt wishes for you happiness had I not been presented first by Mr. Bergman's illness, and subsequently by my own indisposition. As a married wife which I wrote father last week, I begged him to explain this to you.
How much I regret being away at this time dear Hattie. I have so many loving things to say to you which seem so [illegible] when committed to paper. When I received your letter mentioning that you really were to be married my thoughts went back to our past acquaintance then to our growing friendship and intimacy. To all the many many happy hours we have passed together to the kindness that you has always existed between us and which has never been clouded by a doubt on either side and from my own heart dearest Hattie with a prayer that this might always continue and that the friendship that has existed so long much to unchangingly might never while we have been betrothen.
I need not hope that you have chosen a happy destiny. I know you have the [advantage] of so many years as a [happy person] that such is the case and my appreciation of Mr. Johnston's many agreeable

qualities more than support the belief I only wish I have been able [to attend].

...

I learned that you really had decided to be married this winter, but I hope soon ... some obliging might — who will take charge of a party when you have a moment to write me.

Believe me always most truly and affectionately, you sincere friend

Lily Lithe Berghman

ℋℒ

Saratoga Springs[152]
16th September 1868
My dear friend [Harriet Lane Johnston]

Mrs. Roosevelt was just reading your letter dated the 20th of last month and drafted a reply. There was at King's Bend a large bundle of letters from Mr. Buchanan to my Uncle and I hope they may not have been destroyed in the raid which was made on the place ... and shall immediately write to Miss King upon the subject and I will have them forwarded to you ... Among the souvenirs I have two or three letters given to me by my cousin and belong to the package I have maintained. These I will send to you as I return to Ala. Thankful as I have been for Mr. Buchanan's friendship and regarding him with affection as I always did, I take the deepest interest in Mr. Reed's success in the work before him and hope that it will be all that we have a right to expect from an author so capable of fulfilling the trust placed in him.

And I know my dear friend, while your letter pleased it also gave me pain. I have been very remiss in not writing to you since we have parted but for you could hear all the reasons for my seeming neglect you would pardon it. I have been confirmed trials for nearly two years and many troubles were the result of sickness. I knew you were well and prosperous and happy often heard from you incidentally but I had otherwise been in quite ill health and other troubles and had kept from seeking or writing to you. I spent the month of April in medical treatment, and did not know that Mr. Buchanan was ill indeed. I heard he was well. I know beside that had someone informed him of my whereabouts it would subject him to inconsolableness and I hoped with improved health to visit him at Wheatland.

But Man proposes and God disposes of the pleasure of seeing him again was not reserved for me. I can attest to your grief for and bereavement which was no phony one and imagination & often transport myself to Wheatland as it was an visit us.

I went to Richfield Springs with Miss Prince on the 10ᵗʰ of July, and we came here two weeks ago. I have been up and walking about but am far from being well. We go to New York on Saturday en route to Newport.

...

While I was in New York, I called to see Miss. Roosevelt who takes to the world as much as ever, she is very handsome still but large in proportion. Mr. Buchanan's friends are gratified by his kind acknowledgement of her friendship for him. Your little son must be a great comfort to his parents. I am very anxious to see him for me and yours too. If there with you I never saw lovelier brighter with kind regard for Mrs. Shrank. I am ever your friend sincerely

Catherine Ellis

HL

Baltimore July 27ᵗʰ 1870

My dear Mr. Baker

Many thanks for your prompt kindness in the matter of the "Pigs & Lambs." Do me the favor to ship them to Wheatland, advising me there, one day in advance of shipment, and stating at the same time, my pecuniary indebtedness.

I will remember what you say regarding Monsieur Priggs desires and will try to gratify them.

In regard to the Biography, Mrs. Johnston has been of the opinion that $5000 is too limited a sum to secure the services of a proper party, and in a recent letter, Mr. Swarr, on behalf of the Executors, expressed the same views although he proposed what seemed to very impracticable plan of overcoming the difficulty, and one that would probably secure the desired result a <u>century or so hence</u>!!

The only plan is for the necessary capital to be at once contributed by the family in that way alone can their gratitude to their kind and generous relative be manifested.

Mrs. Johnston proposes to unite with Dr. Buchanan, and Mr. Henry in increasing the funds to $20,000.

I need to say that the proposition meets with my hearty concurrence.

It is imminently proper and I am sure all will regard it not only in light of a duty – a <u>sacred</u> duty – but as the greatest of pleasures.

It really is the Ex-President's own money that is contributed. It is a question of justice, <u>not</u> of generosity.

When the fund is raised, I believe under existing relations, that the most expedient of plan is to submit the selection of the Biographer to a committee of political friends of the late Ex President like

O'Conner, Schall, Tilden, Black, or a host of others — men who in common with the whole Democratic Party, have the deepest interest in the book. If it is judged best, let their selection be subject to the approval of the three subscribers to the funds although in my opinion, the whole matter can be more safely left in the hands of the Committee.

The question of the Biography is a very serious one we must try to answer it with the right spirit. It really <u>opens the grave</u> where <u>all</u> can at least for the time, bury their recollections of their wrongs and injuries in order to unite in seeing justice done to the memory of a generous relative, a kind true friend, and a great statesman.

I hope to be at Wheatland by Wednesday next and shall be most happy to see you there.

Do come this time for a <u>visit</u>, and not for a <u>bird's eye view</u>.

Pray, remember me most kindly to Mrs. Black, and to Miss Emily and believe me

Most truly yours

H. E. Johnston

HL

Altoona, September 16, 1870[153]

My Dear Sir [Abraham Cohen Esq.]

Your supposition that the papers which had been in Mr. Reed's hands, had been, before this, placed in a fire proof safe, is correct. They are all now in the vault of the Safety Deposit, Co. of Philadelphia and are in my custody.

I am sorry to have to say that no one has yet been determined upon for the biography. I hope that we may be enabled to selectively secure a suitable person, before long.

With thanks for your kind interest in this matter, I remain respectively yours,

E. Y. Buchanan.

HL

Endnotes

[1] "Has Seen Fifteen Inaugurations," *The Washington Post*, March 3, 1901, Mr. John F. Coyle.

[2] Lily Macalester Collection, Archives and Special Collections, Wadner-Spahr Library, Dickinson College, Carlisle, Pennsylvania

[3] Archives and Special Collections, Wadner-Spahr Library, Dickinson College, Carlisle, Pennsylvania

[4] Ibid

[5] Ibid

[6] Lily Macalester Collection, Archives and Special Collections, Wadner-Spahr Library, Dickinson College, Carlisle, Pennsylvania

[7] Ibid.

[8] Archives and Special Collections, Wadner-Spahr Library, Dickinson College, Carlisle, Pennsylvania

[9] "James Buchanan's Blighted Romance," *The Washington Post*, April 12, 1914, General Isaac R. Sherwood.

[10] Ibid.

[11] Pennsylvania State Archives, Pennsylvania Historical & Museum Commission, Harrisburg, Pennsylvania.

[12] Mark O. Hatfield, with the Senate Historical Office. Vice Presidents of the United States, 1789-1993(Washington: U.S. Government Printing Office, 1997), pp. 181-187

[13] Harriet Lane Papers, Library of Congress, Manuscript Division, Washington, D.C.

[14] Ibid

[15] James Buchanan Collection, Historical Society of Pennsylvania, Philadelphia, Pennsylvania.

[16] Ibid

[17] "Harriet Lane's Load of Wood," *The Washington Post*, February 7, 1892, Page 16.

[18] Harriet Lane Papers, Library of Congress, Manuscript Division, Washington, D.C.

[19] http://www.lanccounty.com/wheatland/

[20] Harriet Lane Papers, Library of Congress, Manuscript Division, Washington, D.C.

[21] James Buchanan Collection, Historical Society of Pennsylvania, Philadelphia, Pennsylvania

[22] Harriet Lane Papers, Library of Congress, Manuscript Division, Washington, D.C.

[23] James Buchanan Collection, Historical Society of Pennsylvania, Philadelphia, Pennsylvania

[24] Ibid

[25] Ibid

[26] Harriet Lane Papers, Library of Congress, Manuscript Division, Washington, D.C.

[27] Ibid

[28] "Harriet Lane's Load of Wood," *The Washington Post*, February 7, 1892, Page 16.

[29] Lily Macalester Collection, Archives and Special Collections, Wadner-Spahr Library, Dickinson College, Carlisle, Pennsylvania

[30] *White House History in James Buchanan's Time,* Journal of the White House Historical Association, Number 12, Winter 2003

[31] *Mr. Buchanan's Administration, On the Eve of Rebellion,* James Buchanan, D. Appleton and Company, New York, NY, 1866.

[32] *White House History in James Buchanan's Time,* Journal of the White House Historical Association, Number 12, Winter 2003.

[33] "Harriet Lane's Load of Wood," *The Washington Post,* February 7, 1892, Page 16.

[34] "Notable Women of Past and Present in Washington's Hall of Fame, E. Ellicott, October 8, 1922, *The Washington Post,* Page 69.

[35] *White House History in James Buchanan's Time,* Journal of the White House Historical Association, Number 12, Winter 2003

[36] "Edward VII and Harriet Lane," reprinted from *The Ladies' Home Journal, Washington Post,* May 5, 1901, Page 27

[37] Harriet Lane Papers, Library of Congress, Manuscript Division, Washington, D.C.

[38] Lily Macalester Collection, Archives and Special Collections, Wadner-Spahr Library, Dickinson College, Carlisle, Pennsylvania

[39] Ibid

[40] Ibid

[41] "Prince's Visit Recalls that of His Grandfather," *The Washington Post,* August 24, 1924, Page 1

[42] "The Prince in Washington, *The New York Times,* October 6, 1860, Page 1

[43] "Prince's Visit Recalls that of His Grandfather," *The Washington Post,* August 24, 1924, Page 1

[44] Ibid

[45] "Edward VII and Harriet Lane," reprinted from *The Ladies' Home Journal, The Washington Post,* May 5, 1901, Page 27

[46] Ibid

[47] Ibid

[48] Ibid

[49] Ibid

[50] "Prince's Visit Recalls that of His Grandfather," *The Washington Post,* August 24, 1924, Page 1

[51] "The Prince in Washington, *The New York Times,* October 6, 1860, Page 1

[52] "Prince's Visit Recalls that of His Grandfather," *The Washington Post,* August 24, 1924, Page 1

[53] Ibid

[54] "Harriet Lane's Load of Wood," *The Washington Post,* February 7, 1892, Page 16.

[55] "Harriet Lane Johnston," *The Washington Post,* July 5, 1903, Page E8

[56] http://www.britannia.com/history/monarchs/mon59.html.

[57] *America's Bachelor President and the First Lady,* 2004, Milton Stern, PublishAmerica LLLC, Baltimore

[58] http://www.dcnr.state.pa.us/stateparks/parks/buchanansbirthplace.aspx

[59] "Buchanan Vindicated — The Charge that He Sympathized with Secession Denied," George Tucker Curtis, Washington Post, May 2, 1883, Page 6

[60] "Personal," *The New York Times,* January 22, 1866, Page 2.

[61] Harriet Lane Papers, Library of Congress, Manuscript Division, Washington, D.C.

[62] Ibid

[63] "The Sorrows of Harriet Lane," *The Washington Post,* November 23, 1884.

[64] "Social and Personal," *The Washington Post,* June 18, 1894, Page 5.

[65] "Our Wealth Widows — Prominent Washington Society," *The Washington Post,* December 9, 1894, Page 21.

[66] "Society," *The Washington Post,* April 22, 1888, Page 4.

[67] "White House Guests," *The Washington Post,* January 12, 1894, Page 5.

[68] "Social and Personal," *The Washington Post,* February 2, 1894, Page 5

[69] "A Blue Room Scene," *The Washington Post,* March 4, 1894, Page 5.

[70] "The Hunt Club Ball," *The Washington Post,* December 29, 1894, Page 5.

[71] "Her Public Reception," *The Washington Post,* February 2, 1897, Page 7.

[72] "In Honor of Victoria," *The Washington Post,* May 25, 1897, Page 7.

[73] "Social and Personal," *The Washington Post,* January 15, 1898, Page 7.

[74] "Notable Gathering at Alibi Club's Annual Tea," *The Washington Post,* December 1, 1899, page 7.

[75] "Events in Social Life," *The Washington Post,* February 3, 1900, Page 7

[76] "Busy Day in Society," *The Washington Post,* May 11, 1900, Page 7.

[77] "For Children of the Poor," *The Washington Post,* January 26, 1901, Page 7.

[78] "Surprise in Society," *The Washington Post,* February 21, 1901, Page 7.

[79] "Tea at White House," *The Washington Post,* December 24, 1901, page 7.

[80] "Busy Week in Society," *The Washington Post,* January 19, 1902.

[81] "Society," *The Washington Post,* May 15, 1902, Page 7.

[82] "Death of Buchanan's Niece," *The Washington Post,* July 4, 1903, Page 1.

[83] "Harriet Lane Johnston Dies at Narragansett," *The New York Times,* July 4, 1903, Page 1.

[84] Last Will, Testament and Codicils of Harriet Lane Johnston, Courtesy of the James Buchanan Foundation for the Preservation of Wheatland, James Buchanan's Wheatland, Lancaster Pennsylvania

[85] Ibid

[86] Ibid

[87] Ibid

[88] http://www.hopkinschildrens.org/pages/residency/history.cfm

[89] Last Will, Testament and Codicils of Harriet Lane Johnston, Courtesy of the James Buchanan Foundation for the Preservation of Wheatland, James Buchanan's Wheatland, Lancaster Pennsylvania

[90] "Choir Boys School," *The Washington Post,* June 1, 1905, Page 11.

[91] "Choir School Dedicated," *The Washington Post,* May 10, 1907.

[92] Ibid

[93] Last Will, Testament and Codicils of Harriet Lane Johnston, Courtesy of the James Buchanan Foundation for the Preservation of Wheatland, James Buchanan's Wheatland, Lancaster Pennsylvania

[94] Ibid

[95] Ibid

[96] "Greater Art Gallery," *The Washington Post,* July 12, 1903, Page 2.

[97] "About the Museum," Smithsonian American Art Museum History, 2004

[98] "$100,000 Statue of Buchanan Lost to City Unless Congress Soon Acts," *The Washington Post,* December 29, 1917, Page 5.

[99] Last Will, Testament and Codicils of Harriet Lane Johnston, Courtesy of the James Buchanan Foundation for the Preservation of Wheatland, James Buchanan's Wheatland, Lancaster Pennsylvania

[100] Ibid

[101] Ibid

[102] "$100,000 Statue of Buchanan Lost to City Unless Congress Soon Acts," *The Washington Post*, December 29, 1917, Page 5.

[103] Ibid

[104] Ibid

[105] Ibid

[106] "Attacks on Buchanan," *The Washington Post*, February 14, 1918, Page 9.

[107] "Wrangle Over Buchanan," *The New York Times*, February 14, 1918, Page 22.

[108] "The Buchanan Statue," Letter to the Editor, *The Washington Post*, February 15, 1918, Page 6.

[109] "Delay for Buchanan Statue," *The Washington Post*, March 20, 1918, Page 7.

[110] "Buchanan Statue Row Is Renewed," *The Washington Post*, June 15, 1918, Page 4.

[111] Records Division of the National Park Service, Department of the Interior, Washington, D.C.

[112] "Hoover at Statue Praises Buchanan," *The Washington Post*, June 27, 1930.

[113] Ibid

[114] Ibid

[115] *The American Presidency Project, John Woolley & Gerhard Peters*, University of California Santa Barbara, 2003.

[116] Pennsylvania State Archives, Pennsylvania Historical & Museum Commission, Harrisburg, Pennsylvania.

[117] James Buchanan Collection, Historical Society of Pennsylvania, Philadelphia, Pennsylvania.

[118] Harriet Lane Papers, Library of Congress, Manuscript Division, Washington, D.C.

[119] Ibid

[120] James Buchanan Collection, Historical Society of Pennsylvania, Philadelphia, Pennsylvania.

[121] Ibid

[122] Harriet Lane Papers, Library of Congress, Manuscript Division, Washington, D.C.

[123] James Buchanan Collection, Historical Society of Pennsylvania, Philadelphia, Pennsylvania.

[124] Ibid

[125] Ibid

[126] Harriet Lane Papers, Library of Congress, Manuscript Division, Washington, D.C.

[127] James Buchanan Collection, Historical Society of Pennsylvania, Philadelphia, Pennsylvania

[128] Harriet Lane Papers, Library of Congress, Manuscript Division, Washington, D.C.

[129] James Buchanan Collection, Historical Society of Pennsylvania, Philadelphia, Pennsylvania

[130] Ibid

[131] Ibid

[132] Ibid

[133] Ibid

[134] Ibid

[135] Lily Macalester Collection, Archives and Special Collections, Wadner-Spahr Library, Dickinson College, Carlisle, Pennsylvania

[136] Harriet Lane Papers, Library of Congress, Manuscript Division, Washington, D.C.

[137] Ibid

[138] Lily Macalester Collection, Archives and Special Collections, Wadner-Spahr Library, Dickinson College, Carlisle, Pennsylvania

[139] Ibid

[140] Harriet Lane Papers, Library of Congress, Manuscript Division, Washington, D.C.

[141] Ibid

[142] Lily Macalester Collection, Archives and Special Collections, Wadner-Spahr Library, Dickinson College, Carlisle, Pennsylvania

[143] Ibid

[144] Ibid

[145] Ibid

[146] Ibid

[147] Ibid

[148] Harriet Lane Papers, Library of Congress, Manuscript Division, Washington, D.C.

[149] Ibid

[150] Ibid

[151] Ibid

[152] Ibid

[153] Ibid

Milton Stern is a writer and editor. He is the author of *On Tuesday, They Play Mah Jongg,* and *America's Bachelor President and the First Lady.* He resides in Washington, D.C.